RADICAL LOVE

An Approach to Sexual Spirituality

Dody H. Donnelly

Dharma Cloud Publishers

Cover Design: Lorraine Capparell

The author gratefully acknowledges permission from the following to use copyrighted material:

The Seabury Press, for excerpts from *New Women/New Earth* by Rosemary Radford Ruether, © 1975 by the Seabury Press.

Mrs. Eulalia Williams, for excerpts from *The Spirit and the Forms of Love* by Daniel Day Williams, © 1981 by Eulalia Williams, originally published by Harper and Row.

The Atlantic Monthly Company, for the poem "A Man and A Woman" by Alan Feldman, © 1975 by Alan Feldman as first published in *The Atlantic Monthly.*

ISBN: 0-9623086-2-5 (previously ISBN 0-86683-817-1)

Library of Congress Catalog Card Number: 92-85514

Printed in the United States of America

2 3 4 5   99 98 97

Dharma Cloud Publishers
P.O. Box 3216
Fremont, California 94539-3216

In memory of my mother
Julia O'Sullivan Donnelly

Contents

Preface

This book is written for us God searchers whose attitude toward living in a body a spiritual life can get in the way of our search—not because we're extra neurotic, but because we are so conditioned that sexuality and spirituality seem like different compartments of our lives that never relate comfortably.

I see spirituality not as some airy laxative that purges the bodily-sexual away, but as the oneness of our human existence lived in the light of faith—a faith that means we know we're loved, and by such a Lover, our God! I see sexuality as the greater intercourse we have with the world, the sensuous embracing of life. That outlook replaces the sensual, compulsive mind that drives us to irresponsible loving.

Sexuality and spirituality are wedded through radical love, a way to be faithful to God's design: the beautiful human person fully alive. This sexual spirituality is a way to see spiritual living as an integral part of the nitty-gritty of bodily, mental, spiritual immersion in God's call to be human. Being holy is an activity for the bedroom as well as the church, because holiness is a human process.

We'll begin by asking, How did we get to this divided way of thinking about ourselves? How can a sexual spirituality centered on radical love heal that schizophrenia? How can that love also cure a damaged self-image and a warped image of God? Next we'll consider the sexual lifestyles that can follow from such a healing love, how they call for moral decisions and the discernment to make them well. Finally, we'll look at the idea of temporary call or vocation, a possible outcome of straightening out our thinking and feeling about ourselves and God. This leads us to look forward to the full functioning of both women and men as God's lovers and as friends to one another, co-responsible with God and one another for the healing of the planet.

Each writer referred to in the text is cited alphabetically in a list of Resources and References at the end of the book in order not to break the text with notes. My sincere thanks go to Martha Wood, my friend and typist, for her constant support, and to my friends Morton Kelsey, Don Gelpi, Malcolm Boyd, Dan Maguire, and Joanne Nash-Eakin who read the manuscript.

Feast of the Epiphany
January 6, 1984

A Look Before We Leap

Before we plunge into our study, let's look at how we got into this place: thinking we have to choose either sex or spirit—but never the two together! It's a fascinating tale of how deeply cultural conditioning could and did shape our present self-image and our image of God.

> Sexuality and procreation correspond to the *lower realm* of corruption, of coming-to-be and of passing away. Redemption demands the flight from corruptibility, symbolized by procreation, to the *immutable (unchangeable) realm* symbolized by virginity.
>
> —Rosemary Ruether

What's the story of the "lower realms" that produced our present schizophrenia? If knowledge is power, then self-knowledge is dynamite. So let's discover how we came to be conditioned to accept these sexual sterotypes that could keep us slaving in the mines of unconscious fear, anger, and guilt.

The story of the division of mind and body is also the story of the malformation of our self-concept, how we think about ourselves, the most important source of our behavior. The self-image emerges from the psychological self and the bodily image, sources of the spiritual aspects of our self-image as well. As we think of ourselves, so will we behave in body, mind, and spirit. Damaging views of one damage them all.

The story we trace affects both women and men, a fact easily forgotten in the present drive for female equality. This sad story reflects the needs and expectations of men; for women—whether pushed by fathers, husbands, sons, clerics, or legislators—learned to be what powerful men insisted they be. Female history is closely entwined with that of males, so the story can enlighten both sexes about our mutual harmful and helpful conditioning by the cultures we passed through.

Until recently, women as a group have made little social

1

progress in influencing their culture because they had neither
the *role models*—real, live, creative, powerful women to imitate—nor the *facts* of their repression to call them to change.
Furthermore, female conditioning forbade women even to raise
their social consciousness.

Charles Ferguson points out that Mary Lyon's founding of
Mt. Holyoke College, the first seminary for women, in 1837
was indeed a revolutionary act. But she was still caught in the
game of meeting male standards of curriculum; hers was neither new nor imaginative, but simply based on that of male
Amherst College. Later, when women finally began to teach in
sacred university halls, they had to follow criteria and curricula
that expressed the values of male faculty and administration.
Today, women *still* comprise a minuscule and scandalous percentage of tenured faculty in American universities.

One hundred fifty years after Mary Lyon, women students
comprise more than half the enrollment of most United States
colleges and universities, but these institutions still often follow
curricula designed by men and for men. It may take years before
women will read books by, hear lectures by, and engage in
intellectual discussions with *equal* numbers of female and male
professors. Today's incredibly low percentage of tenured female
faculty makes equality still a far-off dream.

Men have, of course, suffered from a reverse problem. Too
much control of everything, most of it unaccountable, often
led to corruption. Men suffered, too, from male role models for
whom success was won through violence, aggression, and competition. Men knew little of the facts of their own social history,
because they never saw it through the eyes of the female half of
the race. Women were certainly not the scribes, historians,
newspaper editors, or prime ministers. Nor did they make laws,
set standards, and interpret history, politics, theology, or society's moral norms. Women left pitifully few records for other
women to read.

Slowly recovering the social history of both men and wom-
en, we want to use it for understanding one another, not for
mutual flagellation. Throwing rocks at those who lived before

us wastes time. They, too, were locked into their See-Levels (their world view)—into the Roman fourth century, the Italian Renaissance, or Emerson's New England. Historical data, then, are not weapons, but medicine to heal and tools to change the world into the paradise it can become. As G. B. Shaw put it in *Candida,* "God has given us a world, but only our own folly keeps it from being a paradise."

The human story is the story of our social consciousness, the deepest state of which is mystical prayer or contemplation, opening us to what we feel is ultimate and absolute, God. We have always used symbols to express this inexpressible God. Early Christianity eventually spoke of God as Father, Son, and Spirit.

Before Christianity, woman's body often symbolized the divine; ancient religions found that perfectly natural. The list of goddesses is long—Isis, Astarte, Juno, Artemis, Diana. But Christianity changed all that. In Christianity only one woman was allowed to relate sexually to God: Mary, as *mother* of God, but never herself divine. Women, banished from the godhead, now had to relate to a Mary portayed as immaculate in her conception and as a virgin mother—a difficult model for ordinary women to identify with.

Since we form our self-image chiefly from what family, religion, and society say and do about us, women learned much about their inferiority. Now no longer associated with symbols of God, they hardly thought of themselves as called to heights of holiness. That religious damage was reinforced by philosophies dictating the values of the cultures women had to live in.

One of these, Neoplatonic philosophy, had by the fourth century A.D. become the undergirding for Christian theology's attempt to express theories about Jesus and his relationship to the Creator and the Spirit. Neoplatonism devalued the body as inferior to the soul because body was considered material and therefore less spiritual. Spiritual meant closer to true realaity, which meant some divine idea of human being.

This view was alive and well until recently. Some of us even memorized the catechism answer, "The soul is more important than the body because in losing the soul we lose God and everlasting happiness." Surely, God was surprised by that answer! Theology had by now forgotten its role as theory, especially theory about what it did not completely know: God.

Dualism, this matter-spirit split, won out in the early church. Soon flight from the body became *the* spirituality, the way to live one's faith. To be alone with the Alone, to reject the suspect body as an embarrassing companion, was the real task. Thus developed the spirit. Things have not changed too much. Many of us still believe that when it comes to body and spirit, never the twain shall meet.

Dualism had its roots, however, in *both* paganism and Christianity, with bizarre consequences for woman. The Old Testament saw a woman's body as a particularly suspect body, or as an object, or as property (listed before her husband's other possessions in Deuteronomy 5:21, but after his house in Exodus 20:17). Across centuries woman's body somehow became associated with the material, then with the nonspiritual, then even with the ritually impure. Intercourse with a woman could render impure a priest about to officiate in the Temple. Certainly she herself could never officiate there!

As the Hebrews had fought the pagan goddesses, so the Jewish converts to Christianity struggled with the devotees of the Egyptian goddess Isis and the Phrygian Magna Mater whose cults were pervasive. The most effective rival of Christianity from the second century onward was the cult of Isis; her festival was celebrated with great magnificence.

We cannot, however, equate Old Testament views of women with those of all cultures of the first and second centuries A.D. In fact, the six centuries from Alexander the Great up to the fourth century A.D. were a period of growing liberation of women in Hellenistic culture; the goddess worship was one sign of such change. (In the same way, in twelfth-century France a high point of devotion to Mary as Jesus' mother paralleled the reign of prestigious French queens.)

The first century of the Christian era witnessed a revolution in values, a change from corporate, communal thinking to an individualism so intense that by the reign of Emperor Trajan (A.D. 98-117) Roman society was one in which the individual operated for oneself.

The pagan Rome that spread the principle of equality somehow never lost sight of the concept that all men or women, free or slaves, were by nature equal. The writings of a slave, Epictetus, were read by an emperor, Marcus Aurelius. These ideas were hardly totally put into practice, but they did lead to the gradual emancipation of Roman women. Under Emperor Hadrian (A.D. 117-138) the Roman father lost his power of life and death over his household. Soon he also lost the right to sell his wife or children into slavery. Wives became independent agents. By Hadrian's time women could also dispose of their property by will. By the end of the second century, Roman women were *legally* subjects, but actually free by *custom*.

Juvenal's bitter satire on women, some of Martial's epigrams, and Horace's odes give us pictures of a licentious, free, domineering, and irresponsible Roman woman with her own property, lovers, and lifestyle. Yet, Jerome could find wealthy, educated, intelligent women like Paula for his Bethelehem monastery, because these same centuries gave the patrician Roman girl an education.

Roman women devoted themselves to philosophy, art, philology, literature, politics, and even strategy. Martial's *Epigrams* mention with admiration Roman women who were poets, fluent in Greek as well as Latin. Wealthy women assembled in clubs and busied themselves in philanthropy and social service: they donated temples, theatres, and statues to their towns.

Important for later Christian teaching was the change from marriage as "manus," in which the wife was under the husband's power as head of the family, to "partnership," based on union of hearts and equality of the sexes. Women now had a right to refuse a second marriage partner if chosen by parents. The marriage ritual, the basis of our own, had vows promising mutual self-giving.

On the dark side, fifty-five percent of Roman women entered marriage before their fifteenth year. Naturally the first husband was chosen by parents. A Roman woman's second marriage was self-chosen, and divorce was readily available. Caesar and Antony were married four times, Sulla and Pompey five.

Ancient mythologies had tried to explain what humans observed about each other, including women's biological functions. A woman's body was considered "different" since the male's had become the norm of what it meant to be human. And, of course, basic to all value setting was ignorance of biological data about either sex.

Paleolithic humans did not know, for instance, that male semen was a part of female reproduction—a fact important for the story of the social awareness and the self-images of men and women. Because woman's womb was considered the sole source of life, in many primitive societies she enjoyed respect and even male fear and envy. It was generally believed that the child was formed from menstrual blood that remained in the uterus. But, when we discovered that semen was needed for conception, how then was woman's role explained?

Leave it to the Greeks to answer. In the ultimate putdown, more than three centuries before Jesus, Aristotle, who was a biologist, gave his definitive answer: "Man plays the major role in reproduction; the woman is merely the *passive incubator* of his seed . . . the male semen cooks and shapes the menstrual blood into a new human being."

The later implications of Aristotle's biology proved disastrous for the female self-concept. His thought shaped Christian theology through Thomas Aquinas and the Renaissance and Reformation. Only now is Aquinas' influence beginning to wane. Thanks to such interpretations of women's role, men degraded women further. They even deprived them of dignity by calling them misbegotten males and by claiming the active role in reproduction.

Not until the seventeenth century did the microscope show us spermatozoa in male semen, and not until the end of the eighteenth did we discover the role of sperm. By 1875 the process of fertilization itself had been observed and verified. Incredibly, our present knowledge of chromosomes, gonads, and the equal roles of male and female in reproduction belongs to the twentieth century. But all through the centuries, the proud phallus remained symbol of male superiority and the subordination of women.

The theories used to explain the existence of the second member of our duo, the spirit, often bore equally harmful results for both men and women. The Christian religion, born in the Mediterranean Basin, was affected by Graeco-Latin mythology and philosophy. In creating its theology from Platonic idealism and Aristotelian realism with Stoic overtones, it borrowed theories of how we humans were "enspirited," or living in a spiritual dimension.

We experience the results of such mixed philosophical blessings today in Western law, ethics, and psychology. These show only male-dominated interpretations of physical and spiritual data, because they never included half the experience of the human race: woman's. Thus the male scientist was deprived of vital scientically verifiable input. Woman, deprived of human dignity, never learned to think of herself as equally valuable with man, or as a responsible contributor, coaccountable for the human race—though she coproduced it!

As Christianity began to develop different spiritualities from these mixed philosophical-theological bases, it was influenced by both dualism and the male sexual-identity crisis precipitated by the crumbling Roman Empire. In this time of social distress, the myth of the fall of Adam and Eve in Eden was used to explain evil. The woman, Eve, became the central figure in humankind's disaster! Spirituality became a way to be "saved," and salvation soon meant being saved from woman, the symbol of sex and even of the demonic! So, renouncing evil came to mean renouncing woman. As a mere sex symbol, this inferior female hardly aspired to holiness or to holy priesthood.

Christianity's phenomenal growth after 311 A.D. produced an all-male clergy as Christian women lost any gains in equality made through the treatment of women Jesus modeled in the Gospels. The antifeminist side of Graeco-Roman culture finally won out in the infant church. Influential spiritual leaders cried out against woman:

> You are the door of Satan; you are the one that yielded to
> the temptation of the tree; you are the first deserter of the
> law of God; you persuaded man whom Satan himself had
> not power to subdue; with irresponsibility you led man,
> the image of God, astray!
>
> —Tertullian

What lay behind this pagan and Christian spiritual scorn for
women? Deep roots of superstition and ignorance. Men
puzzled by women's biological processes, had resorted to *magic*
or demon possession to explain their menstruation, pregnancy,
and power to conceive. Soon women were connected with the
dark, dangerous, "evil" dimensions of life.

> The notion that women's sexual processes are impure is
> worldwide and persistent; the magical fear of menstrual
> blood is particularly intense. . . . Blood flowing from
> female genitals . . . sets women off from the other sex
> and gives them the exceptional properties of *mana* in a
> world in which men set the norm.
>
> —H. R. Hays

The writing of the church Fathers fused Gnostic dualism,
Greek philosophy, and cultic purity concepts into an obsession
with the conflict between sexuality and spiritual living. Rosemary Haughton aptly states:

> The Christian teaching about the new life in Christ into
> which the believer entered by faith but which would be
> fully established when the world and the flesh (meaning
> all that is unredeemed and blind in human nature) would
> be overcome, did lend itself to an interpretation that
> emphasized the rejection of physical experience and plea-
> sure, even of beauty, and the exaltation of the spiritual,
> here meaning the non-physical.

Against the rising tide of antisexuality church councils and
writers had to *defend* marriage and procreation—exhorting a

bishop to remain with his wife rather than "pretend piety." Part of this anti-body thrust came from glorification of the life of the hermit and of the new monasticism, often accompanied by the practice of lifelong virginity.

Some Christian writers, especially Clement of Alexandria (d. 215), emphasized Paul's praise of marriage as a way for anyone to be saved: deacon, priest or layperson. But Clement's treatise "On Marriage" was a last Christian cry for balanced sexuality and for the holiness of married relationships before the antisexual wave helped sweep marriage into a secondary spiritual status, at least until the sixteenth-century Protestant Reformation.

However, Clement's treatise also shows how much fear of women was engendered in the Christian Fathers by the claims of women gnostics to teach men or to minister to the community and even to baptize. Gnostic texts emphasize the role of Mary Magdalene. Today women again find Mary's history and mission inspiring and challenging.

No wonder Montanist women were such a scandal to male Christian officials! They reenacted the enthusiasms of Paul's women converts at Corinth. They had to be properly subdued by male power that did not tolerate the notion that a woman could teach a man. This male anxiety was not just because they were women. Rather, it was because they were also prophets, teachers, and apostles. Men just could not see women, Aristotle's "misbegotten males," as thus equally gifted by God.

A series of anti-feminist statements by the Fathers shows how prevalent and strongly entrenched was this image of women as morally inferior. The sexual-identity crisis traced above gives us more understanding of the male's anxiety over self-identity, mirrored in projecting his fears upon the available scapegoat: woman. The same Clement of Alexandria who defended marriage against the gnostics stated that a woman should be covered with shame by the thought that she *was* a woman.

An important factor in the success of the antisexuality wave was the fact that the fourth-century Christian church had now joined the Roman Empire in administering justice, advising rulers, and eliminating paganism and its gods. So Christians, who had once found identity and "salvation" in persecution by that Empire through martyrdom, lost this kind of bloody chance for holiness.

Now that the emperors no longer cooperated, a "white" martyrdom developed as a way to be saved with surety. This white martyrdom was characterized by ascetical practices, mortifying exercises, and, ultimately, freedom from "sexual taint" through celibacy. Ascetic abstinence from sex was supposed to seal the purity of males, now called clerics, on the road to a totally male priesthood.

Clement's view of marriage as a way of spiritual living for clergy and laity alike was replaced in the fourth century by the ideal of a clergy who proved their moral superiority and right to leadership by ascetical abstinence from sexual intercourse.

A fourth-century pope, Damasus, stated that "since intercourse is a defilement, surely the priest must undertake his duties with heavenly aid." Of course, the pope here refers to *legal impurity*, for a priest and not sin in itself. But his letter also says that intercourse was repugnant to the sacred ministry, and that the Scriptures authoritatively required ministers of Christ to live in celibacy (cf. Romans 8:5, 1 Corinthians 7:7). Damasus also asked how clerics could advise perfect continence to widow and virgin if they themselves were not celibate.

Eventually, out of this rejection of the physical came a series of laws of celibacy for clergy. Soon, most monasteries required a vow of celibacy for monks and nuns. The spiritual life was henceforth identified with the nonmaterial, the disembodied, the nonsexual, which meant, paradoxically, the totally male and celibate.

The antisexual obsession triumphed in the works of Western theologians as well. Jerome could see hope for woman only in becoming a man. Augustine of Hippo, whose thinking dominated theology for a thousand years, taught that original sin passed on to children through the act of conception.

Many people fled to the monasteries for spiritual living, some to avoid disastrous economic conditions, but many to escape the "problem" of sexuality.

Yet women found in those same monasteries the dawn of liberation from the stigma society attached to the female body. Melania the Elder, Paula, and Eustochium found in monastic living an intellectual option whose light shines out in their correspondence. Women's intellectual and spiritual life blossomed in the deserts where at one time some 20,000 nuns resided.

Married women of all ranks still found themselves identified with Eve's sin, which seemed to males to be the central point of the Genesis myth. Holiness called for denying sex. Because prayer demanded sexual abstinence, priests called to holiness could never marry. Studies like those of Samuel Laeuchli give detailed explanations of this pro-celibacy.

The half-Christianized medieval period created no new theology to change women's inferior position. Ignorance and long-standing custom only deepened it. Reference to prostitution as an accepted social institution appeared in the writings of Gregory the Great, Isidore of Seville, and Thomas Aquinas, who called the prostitute "a sewer in the palace," a "lawful immorality," "a necessary evil."

This male acceptance of social aberrations like prostitution, typical of both pagan and Christian religions, today continues to damage the sexual maturing of both men and women. Mary's role, as Mother of God whom Jesus had obeyed, led medieval men to find it no dishonor to obey a queen like Blanche of Castile or the famed abbesses of Las Huelgas in Spain.

During the time of the Renaissance and the Reformation, revival of Greek ideas about woman's inferiority reversed even this limited medieval acceptance of women. Thus in 1636 the monks of Fontevrault rebelled against their abbess because the new age found it dishonorable and against nature for a man to obey a woman; such obedience would be against God's law!

Neither Luther nor Calvin carried out for women the liberation from decadent theology they tried to gain for men. Some of that liberation in Christian views of sexuality finally blossomed on English and North American soil, producing some degree of

woman's religious-sexual equality. The Quakers, certain leaders of the Oneida Community, and the Shakers under Mother
Anne Lee gave a woman ordination or its equivalent and even
made her their leader.

How do we move on from such a story? We can decide to
build upon the ruins and reclaim our total humanity *through*,
rather than *in spite of*, being embodied and ensexed. We not
only *can*, we *must*, for we women and men are now together
responsible for the fate of this planet.

Where are we today in our story of this division of body-
spirit, this alienation of male and female? The results of the split
are deeply engrained in North American culture where men
dominate women and human beings abuse the environment.
Eruptions of violence, racism, and sexism are symptoms of an
alienated society and, of course, of a society experiencing the
split between sexuality and spirituality.

In the opening days of 1984, as I finish this writing, the Equal
Rights Amendment has just been defeated in the House of
Representatives by six votes. Power does indeed continue in
male domination. Sadly enough, male success and dominance
are achieved at the expense of the outcast, the poor, and women
and maintained by a system based upon oppression: sexual,
racial, economic, and cultural. Here are some facts that illus-
trate this condition:

• Women continue to be discriminated against in jobs, paid
  \$.59 to every male \$1.00; in medical care; in pensions; in
  credit and insurance.
• The majority of single households are headed by women.
• Women are the fastest-growing poverty group in the USA.
• About 2.8 million women over 65 live in poverty.
• More than twelve million women of retirement age have no
  pensions.
• Four million women between 45 and 65 have no health
  insurance.
• Barely 5% of the tenured faculty in our universities are
  women.

This is a sexual-spiritual disaster area! Jesus Christ asked for an inclusive society of women and men as equals before God, using their gifts to serve the community. So the healing of sex and spirit, of mind and body, is essential for the total healing of society, where both men and women suffer from alienation and the spiritual sickness that follows from sexism, defined as a systemic evil in church and society that always sees woman as unequal and subordinate.

Christianity, because it teaches the ethic of justice and love, must also help end the rule of one powerful societal group, the rich and the male, over powerless people: women, the poor, the nonwhite. Sexuality can no longer be used as a tool to oppress and dominate others in the name of money or religion.

Many women, because of their raised consciousness of oppression, could help men learn a broader definition of sexuality, develop a new self-image, and heal the mind-body split. Sexuality is part of the energy of our relating to other persons as women or men. As sexual beings, we need to think through the meaning of living embodied and to use sexuality *well* as the given ambience of any way we choose to live our faith.

Authentic spirituality takes into account the total life of spirit, soul, and body as the way we see God, self, and others (through the prism of faith). Some of us are still mesmerized by the old fables of a self divided into body and spirit. Inside, we keep telling ourselves about how spiritually inferior we are. Outside, culture and religion tell us about the same thing, implying that holiness can have nothing to do with a healthy sexuality. Now is the time to discard that fable for good and to opt for the *true* story God is always telling us inside—about how good we are, how precious and how loved.

To turn the fable around and to hear God's voice, we need to improve our male/female self-image, and to create fresh images of God. Those two results of the fable—false images of self and God—are the chief enemies of a sexual spirituality that can heal and transform us through radical love.

Becoming aware of the errors of the past will not be enough. A sound theology must also replace an inadequate view of God as a nonsexual somebody—sexless and, so, incapable of relating sexually to us. Because we have deprived God of warm, loving meaning, we have refused to let the real God love us. And how could we hope to love such an "unmoved Mover"? No wonder we were supposed to wait for heaven for "fulfillment"—whatever that meant!

Both sexual and social, then, is a human spirituality that can empower us to love in return a meaningful, loving Thou. Pushing beyond our egos, yearning for meaning and belonging, wanting the reverence that can open us to revelation—all of these aspects of religion are vital parts of *human* experience. If religion is an audacious attempt to experience the universe as meaningful, it needs a spirituality that can then present a meaningful face to the world. Religion does that when it accepts the body, mind, and spirit as all equally beautiful facets of human living.

We must drop, then, the attitude that men are the enemy. "They" must be replaced by "we" if we humans hope to survive. I trust that some ideas in these pages can provide new glasses for everybody, for a God's-eye view of all of us by all of us.

1

Why a Sexual Spirituality?

Sex need not be so urgent, so driven, so mindless, so
concentrated in the genitals. In fact, it seems that *real sex
is only rarely this way.* Usually it is simply not so imperious
or "spaced-out." Sex can proceed in a more leisurely
gentler fashion, with irrelevant thoughts floating through
your mind, with awareness of things other than your
genitals, and with no overwhelming desire to do anything
at all.

—Bernie Zilbergeld

"Sexual" and "spiritual"! They appear worlds apart in popular
parlance. But in the picture of our total humanity what a
oneness they reveal and conceal! Social conditioning has
trained us to see them as almost irreconcilable. Recall how you
learned, over years and experiences, what it was to be sexual, to
be male or female, feminine or masculine. How often did the
pursuit of your sexual identity and your meaning as man or
woman lead to mixed messages about both sexuality and
spirituality?

Too often sex was confused with sexuality itself. To be precise, there is no such thing as sexuality! We've actually never
met a sexuality coming down the hall, have we? But we have
met real women and men who were ensexed, living in an
embodied way called the male or female sex. As ensexed, we
experience our bodiliness; so we can know one more dimension
of ourselves called sexuality. Our bodiliness is the medium that
gives us that sexual message. In a very real sense, we *are* our
bodies and yet more.

Society teaches us differing views of sexuality. One of these is
enshrined in the dictionary. The word *secare* means "to divide,"
and *secus* is male or female sex. Biology tells us however, that

we were *embodied* before we received the gift of *sexuality* or
division into sexes. Genitalia as external indication of sex are
recognizable as male or female only after two months of fetal
development.

This difficulty with assigning one precise meaning to sexuality appears in the four approaches to sex determination and
differentiation that Dr. Robert Lebel proposes:

1. The chromosomal: XX = female; XY = male;
2. The genetic: sex differentiation processes depending on
   the functioning of many genes;
3. The morphological: internal and external bodily structures that identify us as male or female; and
4. The psychosocial: sex orientation or sex-role preference, or way to relate to others as sexual beings.

For purposes of our discussion, we will use "male" and
"female" as biological terms and "masculine" and "feminine"
as *cultural* terms to label how we have been taught to think
about sexuality by cultural patterns of church, family, and
society. Perhaps our attitudes toward these labels will help us
discover how much our attitude toward embodiment can affect
spirituality or the way we picture and respond to God, neighbor,
and self.

I hope our consideration of the many meanings of sexuality
and spirituality can help us to say "sexualities" and "spiritualities." That "s" is vital for a broader view of both that
precludes narrow meanings confining sexuality to genital intercourse, while spirituality is either completely unrelated to sexuality or confined to the celibate lifestyle.

When we do ask ourselves what we think sexuality is and
then check with friends, books, and films, we soon grow aware
of the wide varieties of sexual description. And no wonder, for
each description is lived out by unique persons with much in
common, but also with a world of difference in their temperament, character, and lifestyle.

Out of this human sexual multiplicity come the questions for
both the sex therapist and the spiritual guide. After much

experience these experts tend to agree that the simplistic division of the human race into masculine and feminine (and biologist and geneticist will add "male and female") will no longer wash. These experts see sexuality as deeper and more pervasive than distinctions like external genitalia, ability to reproduce, or attraction to the opposite sex. They insist upon an open, multiple approach to the sexual attitudes of unique people.

Richard Woods talks about the *fourteen* sexes:

> Actually, sexuality is the complex product of at least seven interconnected physiological, psychological and sociological systems differently experienced by males and females, even in the case of a higher mammal. Humanly speaking, there are also specifically *spiritual* elements involved: ethics, religious values, aesthetics, and above *all*: underlying *all*, intelligence and love.

Psychologists like Freud have tended to stress the supremacy of the genital meaning of sexuality, to the detriment of equally valuable affectionate and social dimensions. So we ask the scientists—biologist, anthropologist, and psychologist—what their basic assumption in reard to sexuality really is: Who or what do they think the human person is? All through our journey we'll keep this vital question in mind. Sigmund Freud seemed to assume that the human being was primarily a biological creature. But today's psychology, theology, and spirituality emphasize social and relational aspects, stressing integration and, more important, the primordial oneness of our sex and spirit.

That profound oneness of our being radiates through both sex and spirit. And all the efforts of our culture to the contrary, we do experience that oneness and feel uneasy with the split-level selves we've been taught to accept. Instead of trying to be masculine or feminine according to society's criteria, we could seek a sexual identity not tied to society's stereotypes. We need an awareness of the androgynous, bisexual nature of our human traits.

Professor Jeanne Block of the Institute of Human Development at the University of California has studied these sexual labels, "masculine" and "feminine." She now uses instead the terms "agency" and "communion" to describe these human characteristics that *both* men and women share. She asks for a balance between these two to achieve a mature personality. Block's studies sadly reveal that North American social conditioning has actually impeded such balanced personality growth in our children.

According to Block's terminology, a man should not be considered "feminine" when he is impulsive, loving, sensitive, and sympathetic, but rather a person high in "communion" characteristics. Nor should a woman be called "masculine" if she is ambitious, critical, dominating, rational, responsible, and practical. Rather she is high in "agency" characteristics. Her suggestion eliminates labeling our behavior solely in terms of gender and forces us to recognize the real *likenesses* between men and women in behavior, attitudes, and values.

Behavior
Some Factors Involved in Behavior

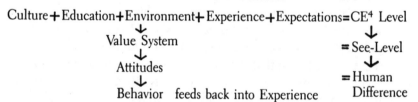

Culture + Education + Environment + Experience + Expectations = CE^4 Level

↓   ↓

Value System   = See-Level

↓   ↓

Attitudes   = Human

↓   Difference

Behavior   feeds back into Experience

The Cycle of Experience:
Dynamic Model of See-Level and Its Influence on Behavior

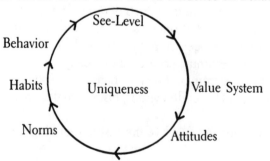

Masculine and feminine social roles came to us through cultural learning and conditioning. From our earliest moments we were influenced to be what parents, teachers, and peers taught us to be: boys or girls. Gradually an identity emerged, molded by the culture, the sexual-spiritual experiences, the environment, and especially the expectations of others. Only with effort did we gradually learn to respond to *our own* expectations.

Those weighty shapers—culture, education, experience, environment, and expectations—make up what I call our "See-Level" (see chart), the very glasses through which we look at our world. We're reading this page through our own particular See-Level, and through it we process everything that comes into our consciousness. Everybody's See-Level, then, includes values—what we cherish, what we feel is worth wanting. Real values are not only what we say we want, but what we actively choose and publicly prize.

When we are not challenged to change, values grow deeper and give rise to our attitudes (predictions) about how we should behave. Characteristic ways of perceiving reality, these attitudes are hard to change. They seldom can be confronted directly, especially attitudes toward sexual identity or toward lifestyles such as homosexuality or bisexuality.

Most importantly, our attitudes lead to how we behave. They involve why we do what we choose to do. Sexual decisions, for instance, have their roots, both conscious and unconscious, in these deeper attitude- motivations. I use this See-Level model to explain where we get our attitudes toward sex and spirit. The most important factor in that model, the *expectations* taught us by parents and peers, helps explain why we are who we are sexually. Yet we know we're still free to change, because at any time God can and does enter our See-Level, initiating help, courage, and love (grace).

When we do change our attitudes in the direction of living our love, we move toward *conversion* or change of heart. Some of us don't change because conditioning has convinced us that so far as sexuality is concerned, change is impossible. So we

give up trying for spiritual growth in the area of sexuality,
especially when our culture provides as our model the current
obsession with "performance."

Performance is a sexual role expectation that pushes us to
value only the genital dimension of sexuality, no matter how sex
therapists try to deliver us from that overemphasis. Pushed to
performance on the basis of inadequate and often fantastic data,
we need to confront that expectation to make wise sexual
decisions. Always we need to ask, Who says so? Is this true for
me? Is it necessarily true at all?

On the basis of such false demands, men and women spin off
on endless rounds of damaging diets and hatred of their own
self-images. In this despairing search for cosmetic beauty and
the fountain of youth, we can end up in that insanity Una
Stannard calls the cult of beauty:

> The obligation to be beautiful is an artificial burden
> imposed by men on women that keeps both sexes clinging
> to childhood, the woman forced to remain a charming,
> dependent child, the man driven by his unconscious
> desire to be—like an infant—loved and taken care of
> simply for his beautiful self. Woman's mask of beauty is
> the face of the child, a revelation of the *tragic sexual
> immaturity* of both sexes in our culture.

So goes the stupid game played by both men and women.
Women are taught to act as if they do not want sex, and men are
taught never really to believe that. Both are caught in
uneasiness and often embarrassment. How is he supposed to
know whether or not she is playing the game? Will she really
comply with his request?

When women do comply (often against their better judgment), men naturally don't seem to believe their future pro-
testations. But women cannot reasonably get angry at their
disbelief, because they have just given men another reason not
to! Alan Feldman's poem "A Man and a Woman" expresses
poignant aspects of that game.

A Man and a Woman
between a man and a woman
The anger is greater, for each man would like to sleep
In the arms of each woman who would like to sleep
In the arms of each man, if she trusted him not to be
Schizophrenic, if he trusted her not to be
A hypochondriac, if she trusted him not to leave her
Too soon, if he trusted her not to hold him
Too long, and often women stare at the word "men"
As it lives in the word "women," as if each woman
Carries a man inside her and a woe, and has
Crying fits that last for days, not like the crying
Of a man, which lasts a few seconds, and rips the throat
Like a claw

       but because the pain differs
Much as the shape of the body, the woman takes
The suffering of the man for selfishness, the man
The woman's pain for helplessness, the woman's lack of it
For hardness, the man's tenderness for deception,
Which is really fear, the man's fear for fickleness,
YET CARS COME OFF THE BRIDGE IN RIVERS
    OF LIGHT
EACH HOLDING A MAN AND A WOMAN!

Yet women are only playing the role they've been taught to play by their own mothers! They were taught to give mixed messages, but not how to deal with the consequences! Bernie Zilbergeld talks about this fantasy model of sex: "It is not a good preparation for the real world. The model ignores the fact that very few women meet the specified criteria of beauty . . . and the man feels inadequate if she does not react as in the best porno films."

Unreal and ridiculous as the performance myth may be, millions of Americans are taught to think of it as sexuality. When we do not realize that this image is fantasy, its unconscious power over us is enormous and we can often project anger, frustration, pain, and guilt in inappropriate ways. When we buy the expectations imposed by this Superperson model of sex, we can feel inadequate and diminished by our personal sexual expressions. Awareness of this harmful pressure from expectations can be the beginning of liberation from its destructive effects.

Learning wider, liberating meanings of sexuality can counteract that performance syndrome. So we start by examining who we are, a point we will also consider later when we examine how our self-image is formed. Then we ask what God may have to tell us about the "performance" sexual model. Daniel Maguire emphasizes these psychospiritual aspects of sex: "Sex is not ecstasy without a mission. Psychologically, it is a sacrament of intimacy leading to self-revelation, trust, and friendship; it is unitive."

Maguire points out that for human beings sex is not just an instinct of reproduction but a highly symbolic act with tremendous psychological meaning. Sex certainly can, and often does, meet physical needs and relax nervous tension, but it is also a mighty symbol. Sex can express profound emotion, self-giving, and the deepest human meanings because it is an intense form of sharing that invites even more openness.

Sexual sharing is beautifully symbolized by physical nakedness. Nakedness is a convenience, yes, but it means more than physical openness to one another. It shows willingness to share also the psyche (the mental dimensions of our souls), the spirit, the total self. And if sexual union is to mean the growth of personality, it will be a sign of respect, love, and valuing. Significantly, these qualities are generally associated with friendship, the highest form of cherishing we humans know on earth. As we shall see, friendship may well be the key to human sexual-spiritual maturity.

Sexuality is socially meaningful, too, and therefore an indication of the cultural level of our civilization. At its deepest level, sexual union involves the union of two personalities, so it can never be without social meaning. Most importantly for growth in spirituality, sex gives us an index to our personal human attitudes. In sexual behavior we reveal the uncensored self.

Sexuality and spirituality totally pervade our lives. Most

problems of relating the two come from either exaggerating or underestimating this fact. To avoid exaggeration, we need to see that sexuality is only *one* dimension of human personality, one way to express who we are by what we do. The person as "body-self" in its social reality is larger than sexuality. Therefore, gender or sexual roles are vital factors of personality, but they can never speak for our total selves. So "person" is rightly prior to sexuality, and we as human agents need to move on to responsible choices. Underestimating sexuality means repressing or denying its beauty and power as an integral part of us as developing humans.

We learners, conditioned yet free, are always, first of all, persons. Above all, we are responsible agents who know, love, and decide to act. We don't experience ourselves as solitary sex drives divorced from our psychosocial, spiritual selves. No pat answers about sex await us "out there." Rather, each of us, helped by friends, community, and our religious traditions, needs to make sound sexual choices. We are truly our own parents as we birth our sexual-spiritual selves.

It is difficult for us to learn how to discern sound sexual decisions and carry them out, but such decisions can eventually help us to grow in love and to avoid haste and fear. Discerning also implies that we're honestly searching for the true meaning of our own personal sexual behavior. It asks us to be accountable to self, others, and God.

Daniel Day Williams emphasizes that need for honesty:

> We share sex with the animals, but for us the organic urges and acts are never detached from the search for meaning, whether successful or not; it is the selfs search for belonging through communication with another, so sexual attraction in itself is a fleeting indicator of what sexuality is.
>
> The question always is in all human sexual attraction: What use will you make of me? What do you want, what do you expect of me? Are you exploiting or loving me?

We are shaped by our culture, yes, but as free creatures we're still clearly responsible for our sexual-spiritual decisions. We face a considerable task: to learn to use our unique endowment of sexual- spiritual being through, and not just in spite of, our limitations and strengths. Our task is to reclaim in our time our intrinsic oneness and thereby heal our present sad separation of body and spirit, of men and women.

The human enterprise is exploration into God; and we find God in recovering God's *total* gift to us. God's gift is not a divided sex and spirit, but a sexual spirituality that can heal our hearts and, in the process, heals our world as well. At one with ourselves, we can bring peace to this divided world. Each of us is called to contribute a vital part to that exciting enterprise. With Nikos Kazantzakis, we cry out:

> And I strive how to signal my companions . . . to say in time a simple word, a pass-word, like "Conspirators"; let us unite, let us hold each other tightly, let us merge our hearts, let us create for Earth a brain and a heart, let us give a human meaning to the superhuman struggle.

In order to prepare ourselves for that conspiracy to create for earth that brain and heart, we have explored the roots of the warped conditioning that left us so divided into stereotypes like sex and spirit. Now we will consider love as the dynamic power of sexual spirituality—a spirituality that lives its faith by accepting and giving God's passionate love. Love at its depth means the giving of faithful devotion to another on terms that do not threaten or corrupt that devotion. Daniel Day Williams in his *Spirit and Forms of Love* says that "Christianity in its essence does not look upon sex as something that belongs to the lowest part of human nature, but as a power that leads to one of the highest forms of communion."

In fact, Christianity set up the vision once and for all: "There is neither slave nor free, there is neither male nor female; for you are all one in Christ Jesus' (Galatians 3:27-28). That's Paul's way of saying what D. D. Williams means by "a power that leads to one of the highest forms of communon." Ultimately, when it is responsibly, lovingly used, sexuality can lead to that *oneness in Christ*, the goal of all our striving.

2

To Love Is to Be—Human

Every act and gesture is a word spoken. We are not . . .
over-spiritualizing our view of sex when we say that every
sexual act, feeling or emotion has the power to become a
disclosure of spirit to spirit. Sexuality is never something
by itself. It is always a meaning incarnate.
                                    —Daniel Day Williams

Spirituality, fashioned from our personal theory of who we
think God is, describes how we live out our love affair with
others and God through our unique See-Level. Women, not
permitted or not encouraged to study theology, have always
practiced spiritualities based on male theories of who the holiest
people were supposed to be—usually male saints. But even
people who studied theology were not taught that theology is
only theory about the experience of God's loving touch. More
often theology meant studying dogmas (beliefs) and passing
these theories on—including theories about how to love and be
loved—unchanged and unchallenged.

Deprived of means to express their religious experience (a
theology), women could not enrich us with their insights into
how they prayed and practiced their faith. With rare, beautiful
exceptions like Teresa of Avila and Julian of Norwich, we lost
valuable descriptions of what women thought spirituality meant
and how women saw God. So Christians went on only half
understanding God and themselves, deprived of fifty percent of
the human perspective: women's.

So today "cleaning up our language" (eliminating the use of
exclusively male words in worship, writing, and speaking) is not
a feminist fad. Modern inclusive language is an outward sign of
the full acceptance of women as daughters of the church. It
increases women's sense of worth and improves their self-

image. It also helps the whole church, for it helps heal our male and female separateness.

We know that language shapes perception. All of us, both women and men, need to hear ourselves named God's beloved in all the language of both church and society. "Person" means we are open to others and to meaning that always tries to go beyond the ego to more meaning. We search always for some "thou," some meaning carrier and for an ultimate Someone as well. We search because we are being sought by a God who never stops initiating love. We respond to that love in our yearning for more meaning. We try to burst our egoistic bonds as we see the challenge to reject the false "godlets" we may be worshipping: position, beauty, money, sex, power.

Faith means saying Yes to God's loving touch and enables us to respond to that loving. So spirituality mirrors how we respond to and image God. Spiritual growth, then, has to do primarily with how much we allow God's expectations to shape and teach us. And God's is one kind of conditioning we need never resist, for God can be trusted to move us in the direction of our full humanity.

Faith is a process that makes us grow as we respond to God through prayer and the other actions that feed faith. No role, no place, no time can keep us from becoming God's friends once we accept God's love. Freedom as the right to choose means we are still responsible for our choices. So spirituality will call for choices that use our freedom to become God's friends.

But before discussing friendship, we need to clarify what spirituality is. A fuzzy word that rapidly became a fad, spirituality is simply the way to live faith. It was applied to historical models like Franciscan, Methodist, and Jewish spiritualities. Culturally conditioned, they were all colored by specific centuries or special persons—Luther, Francis of Assisi, Maimonides, Wesley. We probably share in one or more of those traditions.

Each of us at this moment also has a personal spirituality shaped by the expectations and teachings of our local communities. Any way to live faith, any spirituality worth its salt, unifies; it harmonizes the dimensions of our total personality. Traditionally, religions have pointed to God as the most potent harmonizer of the human beings that we are—in all the dimensions of God's design.

Because spirituality involves how we act, it comes from our See-Level and what we value as deepest priorities. So what do we value? Beauty? Power? Love? Goodness? Money? Friendship? Because each See-Level is unique, our spirituality can be hindered by our trying to copy someone else's or by comparing our virtue with theirs. A major trap in spiritual growth is neglecting to develop our own unique potential.

God's are the expectations that we want to shape us as we journey after the meaning of our uniqueness and difference and how to accept and live it. Many times we ask, "What is life all about?" Yet, all the while, life is really saying to us, "There is only one of you. What are *you* about?" Our spirituality lives out the answer to that question in the light of faith.

Sound spirituality is essentially social as we pursue our answers, for we need other people to grow. The Christian God we meet in revelation and Scripture is so delighted when we humans love one another! John says that if we say we love God and hate our neighbor, we are liars (1 John 4:20). How thrilled is the heart of the Mother-Father-God when the children love one another!

This God also teaches us to deepen our joyful understanding of who we are to Him: beloved. Because we are so loved, part of developing spiritually is learning to accept the human condition with its strengths and weaknesses as embodied, ensexed, enspirited lovers.

Certain spiritualities in the past emphasized perfection as the one way to relate to God. Seeing the consequent damage to our self-concepts today after centuries of perfectionism, I say, "S.O.P., Stamp Out Perfection"—the kind of perfection that means no mistakes, no sins. *Per-fect* means "done all the way through *for you*," with your unique See-Level! God is not upset about our imperfection; *we* are!

For example, if we bake a batch of cookies and someone

wants to throw them all out except one, because only that one is the "right" shape, we protest loudly! Yet we keep trying to measure up to some heavenly cookie shape we think God (or some friend) wants for us, when all the while we ourselves *are* the unique one God cherishes—a perfectly good cookie! By accepting God's love, we can accept our own uniqueness and use it to love and serve.

The question is, Will we accept responsibility for this unique custom model we are, and stop comparing ourselves to others? Comparing may be a cop-out. If we see others who seem holier in their form of spirituality, we give up. We stop trying to pursue our own identity or live up to it, or forge a valid personal spirituality with our particular gifts, or even learn to pray our own way.

Responding to God with our lives is both the way and goal of prayer. Yet, prayer is not necessarily saying many words. When we use someone else's words to pray, that's vocal prayer, a solid kind like the "Our Father." In vocal prayer, we try to *mean what we say.* And in mental prayer, we try to *say what we mean* in our own words. The practice of the disciplines of meditation, prayer, contemplation, and service helps foster the flame of faith. These practices teach us the meaning of who we are, sexual- spiritual lovers.

But prayer is sometimes frightening because it means that we have to step into the ring—the ring of light of God's gaze, where we can't hide. We can't help dreading prayer, because in honest prayer we might meet God. And we are afraid of two things if that should happen: (1) God may turn out to be Someone different from our fancied image; and (2) we may turn out to be somebody different, too.

Yet if we give ourselves the chance to meet God each day for at least fifteen minutes alone and in peace, that fear will subside. In that encounter we do not pray hard so that God will hear us. Rather, we pray hard so that we can hear God teaching us all we need to know.

It is so important in our personal prayer to get in touch with who God is. The real God wants to teach us to enlarge our horizons and to correct false images of God that may lurk in our minds, for we all have these images and only gradually discard them. Relating to this "constructed God" in our heads can be a major obstacle to meeting the real God who wants to meet the real us. The more we can admit who we really are in prayer with God, the more God can reveal God's self to us. God wants an appointment with the real person we are: God's beloved.

As we free ourselves from false images of God, we pass beyond thinking about God to experience religious feeling. We begin to love God with our emotions, as well as with our minds. At the core of religious feeling is its power to lift us out of ourselves and set us in the living presence of God loving us through those very feelings.

So we learn about God's yearning for us in delightful breakthroughs that are never in our control but always perfectly timed by God. Of course, our bodies can be deeply involved sexually in that loving, as God chooses.

"I love a Mystery" is the theme song of the human heart, because this God we are falling in love with in prayer, the One we pursue, is Mystery itself, fascinating and fearful. God is mysterious, not because we cannot understand God, but because God is so different from us.

Prayer, as a vital activity of sexual spirituality, deepens our consciousness of the pulsating, never ending seduction God carries on in our hearts. Prayer gives God equal time in our lives. The heart of prayer is accepting our dependence on God, a dependence that dignifies us because of the dignity of the Lover on whom we depend.

In the prayer of great mystics this consciousness of God's loving presence is intensely alive, sometimes accompanied by phenomena like ecstasy, rapture, even levitation. And these are the "sweets" of prayer, the paraphenomena of religious experience. They're not necessarily indications either of God's presence or of our holiness. The greatest mystics, like Teresa of Avila, ask us to disregard these states and concentrate on the "ordinary" [sic] object of religious feeling: God loving us! Like children watching a circus, we must be taught to ignore these extraordinary "elephants" of emotional experience in all their panoply and learn to feast our gaze on God, the great Lover they carry.

God has deep lessons to teach us in prayer. The most important is how to love, and the most difficult is how to accept love. But what does love, that overused word, mean? For Augustine of Hippo in the *Confessions,* human love meant experiencing his friend's life as his own:

> And since I was his other self, I wondered the more that I could go on living when he was dead . . . . For I felt my soul and his to have been one soul in two bodies. And so I dreaded life because I did not want to live mutilated. And so, perhaps, I dreaded death, lest the one I greatly loved should die entirely!

This aspect of oneness in the experience of friendship is a most revealing sign of what Jules Toner calls "radical love."

> It leads to seeing into the heart of love. In this experience I'm neither projecting my life into the other, and so at root loving myself in him/her . . . nor losing hold on my own distinct and unique self-identity . . . . when the loved one's life is experienced as mine, I become both more keenly alive to my own distinct self, and reverently alive to the other in his distinct otherness . . . participation in the beloved's life *is in direct ratio to the intensity of radical love.*

A beautiful thing follows from that experience. When we identify with the ones we love and yet permit them to remain their unique selves, we don't swallow them, or own them, or ignore their personhood. In other words, we move toward friendship.

In friendship we participate in our lover's life in direct ratio to our love for them. Yet, we also love friends enough to let them remain distinct and unique. Then, we have an equality and possibly "love." But, more of friendship later, as we here consider love's goal.

According to Toner's idea of radical love, we are *in* the one we love as different from us; yet our love makes us more fully ourselves. The consequences for our society would be staggering if we understood and lived this insight. Dante says that when I love you I "in-you-me." When we share such uniqueness while we retain otherness, how can we *not* see each other before God as deeply bonded, no matter what our sex? Are not all of us, male and female alike, glorious different "showings," "breakings-forth" of God's love in the world?

When Jules Toner quotes Erich Fromm's definition of love, he disagrees with Fromm's meaning of *union*. For Toner, the union that is love demands presence as the vital factor; that can happen only through mutual knowledge and love. Being present as the one known and loved is not the same as being present as the one doing the knowing and loving. Why? Because being known and loved is a way of *being-in* the one doing the knowing and loving as a *receiver* of love, as the beloved.

The radical love that leads to union of beloved and lover demands feelings of mutual presence. Radical love makes us present to one another in many different ways: (1) by mutual knowledge and (2) by physical (sexual) or spiritual union. Radical love, then, is a profound way to live our sexual spirituality by mutual sharing of our lives.

But what is it we actually do when we love? Love has to do with a feeling response, with self-giving, and with presence. Love is actually *being in* the loved one; it is also the gift of self, for the lover is in the beloved as a gift. So radical love is an act by which lover becomes gift to beloved while accepting their otherness, their radical difference, their right to be themselves.

Radical love is not giving the beloved *something* of the self. Rather, it is giving the *total* self, for we ourselves are *in* the loved one by our love, "not merely by our possessions nor even our thoughts . . . [but] ourselves," says Toner.

If we humans are ever to discover a truer meaning for sexual love, we need to begin by acknowledging the legitimate role of *eros* in sexual human spirituality. Rollo May says, "*Eros* is the drive toward union with what we belong to—union with our possibilities, with significant other persons in our world in relation to whom we discover our own self- fulfillment."

Eros is always alive; sexual desire is not. "Sexual desire without *eros* is primarily a fact about ourselves. United with *eros* it becomes a fact about the beloved," says James Nelson in *Embodiment.*

Honesty urges us to admit that we do not yet fully understand human sexuality. Honesty asks us to listen to the body as teacher just as valuable as the mind. Honesty also asks us to face the ambiguity of certain labels like "man" and "woman," given the questions biology and genetics ask today about these once clear distinctions. Because the human reality of men and women lies *in nature itself,* and not in words or abstractions, terms like "male" or "female" may prove less than helpful in our modern journey toward a sexual spirituality.

True liberation from that sexual-performance syndrome that calls for some ideal male or female performer will take heavy work, for honesty demands we look at real individuals as unique women and men and not as males and females. And so far we have learned to relate in a delightful variety of ways. Marriage, now in dry dock for repairs, names only one way to so relate. Perhaps its present distress will be incentive for us to think of other fulfilling, loving ways to relate. After all, it is the mutual love in sexual spirituality that legitimates the holiness of marriage as friendship, and not vice versa. Marriage is not an end in itself or necessarily a state that makes holy.

The present sensual culture found in U.S. media cannot accept the spiritual meaning of sexuality. It distorts it, does it violence, idolizes it (pornography), and demeans it (puritanism). What it will not do is look honestly at the body's lessons, its challenge to become fully human, whole, and creative like its Designer. So compulsive minds drive our bodies into every kind of sickness, physical and psychic.

Genitality divorced from the whole divine choreography
of sexuality must become twisted, stunted and grotesque.
Like anything cut off from the divine source of life, it will

require ever greater satisfactions and stimulations in order to sustain its illusion of life and existence, its forgery of true being.

This frenzied thirst for life will become a demonic drive toward more and more genitality to the exclusion, ultimately, of everything else. And one will have arrived at the great loneliness that is sin, apartness from God, the source of true being. It is the exclusion, and one's attendant withdrawal from the vast social-sexual life of creation in dialogue with God that is evil; it is not genitality in itself. But because the spirit has failed . . . to direct genitality to its proper role in the dance of creation, *genitality is sinned against.*

—James Deschene

Sexuality can carry us beyond itself to become a part of the highest human virtue, love. The Christian church claims that the heart of its teaching is the doctrine of love, of *agape,* a New Testament word for love: "Love is patient and kind; love is not jealous or boastful" (1 Corinthians 13:4). Paul's *agape* is not a refined, nonmaterial, spiritual elixir, some otherworldly ambrosia.

Agape does not come to human love merely as a rescue operation when fidelity fails and reconciliation is needed. The need for the love that gives faithfulness pervades the whole sexual experience.

We say the *need* for *agape* because we are often far from realizing or accepting its presence. It can make itself known as need long before we know its creative healing power.

The Christian affirmation that the love of God and neighbor is the foundation of life can be discerned in the mystery of sexual love that leads persons out of themselves into a new dimension of love.

—Daniel Day Williams

Sexual love can serve *agape.* Not that we can't make love

unless we're thinking about serving God—but the learning from sexual love can make it a graduate school that fleshes out love for God and empowers us to serve and love better! In the very act of making love, two people can love, thank, and adore God. The drive for union fulfilled in sexual love can be part of the transcending of the ego we experience trying to love God spiritually. Spirituality must be sexual if it is to be *human* spirituality! We love God either as ensexed and embodied creatures or not at all. We love God as humans who are men and women all the time in everything we do.

Why do some people want to keep the Spirit (God) in the parlor while making love in the bedroom? The best sources seem to suggest that God likes bedrooms, too. In fact—can we possibly emphasize it enough?—God *invented* the bedroom's activity. So making love can celebrate God's creativity in our own design as human lovers.

So little time and energy have been devoted to the study of love of any variety that we know more about nuclear reactors than we do about either sexuality or spirituality. Sexual love has been something to feel guilty about; it's so natural and earthy! And it's also the cause of so much pain and guilt. So why study it? What's there to learn?

The project is not to turn *eros* (sexual love) into *agape*, especially in making love, nor to feel guilty if we do not succeed. Making love as cherishing is already a holy exercise, for the human act of sexual intercourse happens to be God's design. So when we give ourselves freely to one another physically in love, we act with God, loving God and one another. We thereby share in the creative energy of the universe, the life force, and thus in God's loving energy and plan.

Agape, associated with relationship to God, is another way to talk about the drive to union, and another expression of our humanity. *Eros* and *agape* are not divorced either in head or heart. They merely label differing descriptions of making whole, of the drive toward union with human or divine Lover.

Paul in 1 Corinthians 13 gives us some insight into loving. He situates what I call radical love in *agape*, which for Paul is not

some spiritual brand of love. As self-giving, it is enriched as it
transforms our loving through the union of lovers. *Agape* never
need exclude sexual love; indeed it incorporates it validly into
spirituality. *Agape* asks us to be responsible for our own and our
lover's integrity. As mature caring, *agape* like *eros* helps forge
our sexual spirituality:

> *Agape* is distinguished . . . in that it is not dependent on
> the attractiveness of the object, doesn't include a desire to
> possess him, and need not be in the least sentimental. It is
> supremely an authentic concern for the other . . . his
> integrity. But such a love can't exist without a dimension
> of accepted judgment which is actually a part of this love
> itself.
>
> If my love for my fellow human is to be *agape*, it must
> be this person in his authenticity I love. If I don't see him
> as he is, but have covered his reality with a facade of my
> prejudices, wishes or fears, then my feeling is not *agape*,
> since it's not concern for him *as he really is*—it's concern
> for an entirely spurious individual whom I've invented
> and substituted for the real one.
>
> —Douglas Fox

Exciting for the notion of sexual-spiritual friendship is
Toner's reminder: Accepting the beloved means that they're
present in us not only by *their* desire but also by *our* accepting
them. So they become doubly loved. Our mutual desire, our
living in each other, is union of being. It creates identity
between us. So radical love's feeling dimension makes us one in
a truly sensuous experience involving our God-given senses as
they were made to function—in delight!

The loving we do each day is as ordinary and as miraculous
as the sunrise, and as taken for granted. Perhaps we believe we
really understand it because we experience it. But it remains a
mystery. Teilhard de Chardin calls love "the most universal,
formidable and mysterious of cosmic energies," a hint about its
hidden powers.

Yet we must clarify love as much as we can. Radical love can help us to accept our embodiedness as an essential ingredient of spiritual love because it accepts the total humanness of my lover. If our love is the spontaneous response of caring, it can make us truly one and truly human. Radical love as vehicle of sexual spirituality is a psychospiritual, embodied process that heals our total selves. To understand that love is the primary human task, a task that takes years and tears, but no learning is more precious.

> Real love is effective. If you really love, you do something about it, and do it as well as you can manage to learn how, whether prayer, sex, or revolution. Perhaps the most successful anti-love device of our clever culture has been this separation of love from technique . . . technique means know-how, accurate knowledge . . . about how human beings are, what people are like and how they develop.
> —Rosemary Haughton

3

Falling in Love With God

In a church racked by fears of sexuality . . . the message
that we most need to hear is from the life of Jesus . . .
who sets up no sexual lifestyle as superior . . . either
marriage or celibacy, hetero-or homosexuality; a person
who can be intimate and tender with men and women,
but, most of all, a person freed from obsession with the
sexual as sexual, because his relationships were controlled
not by sexuality but by friendship.

—Rosemary Ruether

The great books of various religions give differing accounts of
how the divine and the human can relate in love. The Christian
Scriptures teach that Jesus Christ claimed a unique love relationship to the God he called Father. The God we humans
spend our lives trying to get into our butterfly nets Jesus simply
called "Daddy" (Abba).

When we try to live as Jesus did, to take on his values and
attitudes, we are in the business of loverhood, trying to be lovers
as Jesus was. The central message of his teaching was loving
and, especially, accepting God's love. His last message to us was
to love as he loved us, and as his Father loved him—freely!

To love Jesus' way, we learn (and are taught) to let ourselves
be seduced by God through loving one another. So sexual love
can never be downgraded because we need its energy to help us
live out Jesus' values and to harmonize our human powers for
loving one another through serving. We also need to learn to
love through valuing our own presence as gift.

Our spiritual love for God, from God, and from others is
influenced by the fact that we live and love through our bodies
as an integral part of our total psychospiritual selves. Whether
being male or female makes a difference in the kind or quality of

that spirituality is not the question here. (At this point in women's social evolution, I believe that it does.) But our love for each other is certainly shaped by our sexuality, since our bodies—our hands, our limbs, our selves—are the joyful means we use to express our caring and concern!

If we accept God's love, we also accept our embodiedness, because God happens to love us as sexual, embodied humans. That acceptance begins the healing of the dualistic split of mind and body. We can now think of our bodies as vessels for God's love. We are embodied receivers for God, but as we shall see, we are also *active* lovers. Falling in love with God, then, asks that we both love and surrender, letting go to God's loving seduction. Jules Toner's dynamic of love helps light up this process of a sexual-spiritual love for God. Presence, you recall, is a coexistence, a being with and in the lover, physically and psychically through knowing and spiritually through affection, feeling, and identity. This love is union of presence, not just the tendency to union but a being-affection: "The being-affection that I call radical-love is itself an act of being-in-union that presupposes knowing and loving the beloved and that makes possible a deeper union of knowledge."

Love as an act of "being-in-union" means vibrating in harmony with the beloved's life. Love means welcoming the beloved into our lives and making our two lives one. Thinking alike and learning how to share flow from that union of presence.

The mystery of human love is microcosm and symbol of love between God and us, so why not also of love within God's own life? If when we love we actually participate in the beloved's life and experience it as ours (yet theirs), then we make a gift of our lives to them. The beloved in turn receives, cherishes, and reciprocates our being part of them.

At work here is a fascinating dynamic that must happen before this miracle of presence can happen. Sebastian Moore feels that to understand human love, or God's, we must consider the dynamic of falling in love. First comes attraction to the lover. Then gradually we feel a growing desire to be someone for them, someone special.

When my lover learns of my attraction and responds with the incredible surprise of accepting my love, then suddenly our original desire for one another grows by leaps and bounds! Our love moves into a new stage. We now live in one another as known, accepted, and cherished.

Moore warns that we cannot understand love unless we observe this process carefully, because this is precisely the point where love tends to give the theologian and philosopher the slip. We assume that love is a feeling of one person for another; we forget that my beloved's response to me is just as essential as my feeling for the miracle of oneness to burst through our separate selves.

When we compare this dynamic of human love with God's love, the project may seem hopeless. God seems too far away and too perfect for me to love or to feel his response. Or God seems like a Sunday School teacher living in the church basement most of the week. How much is our mental picture of God something like that? Such an image can hide from us the real God who Augustine claims "has a passion for us." What a different image that is!

Sometimes we may feel, too, that we can't learn how to love God—not just because we're not holy enough but because there's no natural connection between us. "God's in his heaven, and we're stuck in the world," may be our theme song. But our *connection* with God is already started. At this moment, deep within us God draws us close. As we surrender to that love, we soon experience that God has first loved us. That adverb "first" is one of the most important words in the entire Scripture. God has always been loving us, for God's song is "I Can't Stop Loving You."

God tells us every moment—if we will only listen—that we are someone for Her. Our own desire for God operates, often unconsciously deep within us, as our capacity for receiving God's love. Otherwise, God would not be a lover, but some caretaker, some Big Daddy Warbucks in the sky beaming sunshine on the little humanoids.

Throughout this book I sometimes call God She; sometimes, He, not because God is either (we just don't know that about God), but because this inclusive language demands that we expand our sometimes totally masculine image of God to include the feminine as well. We must let God be what/ whoever God is and not only what our culturally conditioned God has always been: male. Let this change of pronouns impinge upon your consciousness, let it happen to you as you read. See if it might broaden your picture of God, sometimes with surprising inner results!

No matter how we name God, She operates deeply, constantly within us. All that's true, beautiful, loving, and good in us is the shining out of our innate desire for God. This radar yearning for God, the homeland of our souls, was installed long ago in the journey of our spirit.

When we hear the good news that God has *first* loved us, the spark of yearning within us bursts into flame. We now have permission to respond, to expand that love forever, because we are loved and by such a One! Now we hasten to accept that love.

Some theologies in the Christian story have called that initial, first love of God for us the forgiveness of sin. Most incredibly, that outpouring of God's love is a giving and receiving of *persons* in love, sometimes accompanied by our tears of grateful joy as God satisfies our thirsty hearts.

Now we can see the importance of a radical love that shares in the beloved's life as our own. For that is just what happens when we let God participate in our lives. *God's life* becomes ours, too! Still God's, but also ours, as God forever sustains and nourishes us, gently drawing us closer to Himself. Yet God, as perfect gentleman/lady, lets no love affair begin until *we* decide to respond to God's wooing, until we say Yes to being someone for God. Once we say Yes, our real human adventure begins.

God's love, like human love, is now in us as gift. Some theologians have called that gift the Holy Spirit, the divine Breath, that in every way keeps us alive. No "sloppy *agape*," this love is life itself.

When God loves us and we accept that love, then we too are

in God, our Beloved, as gift. And we are in God, our beloved, as an accepted, cherished, longed-for gift, as God's beloved! We have only to say Yes. "The Spirit and the Bride say: Come! and we who hear, answer: Come! Come, Lord Jesus!" (Revelation 22:17, 20). We simply say Yes to God's yearning love. To accept God's love is the deepest practice of faith.

But can loving this God have anything to do with our living embodied or with sexual love? Our answer depends upon who or what we think God is and who we think we humans are. How can we separate our embodiedness from God's total loving? God loves us as human, in our bodily form, in which God somehow sees his own image. The designer hasn't given up on his product. God has waited for centuries for the message of Jesus to get through to us: "You are loved," He says, "just as you are— physical, sexual, embodied, and enspirited. I love you passionately, spiritually, totally; for I am Life and Love itself."

Learning to see the mystical nature and the holy meaning of sexual union opens us to the notion that God touches and delights our embodied selves in whatever way She chooses. People who have experienced this total holistic love of God are free in our present mystic period to express in artistic form a theology of *eros*, needed for so long in church and society. A theology of *eros*, of sexual love, along with one of *agape*, hastens the healing of body and spirit, men and women, God and us.

Poet William Everson powerfully presents such a theology of *eros*. Not only has he experienced the mystical nature of sexual union, but he also has the gift of expressing it—as in his "River-Root/A Syzygy":

> What quickened (this poem) was the intuition that if sex
> was finally going to be expressed openly in this pluralistic
> society, then its religious and contemplative dimension
> ought to be established at the outset; that the new wave of
> consciousness must be sourced in authentic impulses.

In the outpouring of his erotic poetry, Everson is in the direct line of Ramon Lull's *Book of the Lover and the Beloved*, and the Bible's "Song of Solomon." Everson succeeds in his endeavor to establish the religious, contemplative dimension of sex.

Where the phallos
Kisses the womb-nerve listening
The Father is.
And the Father and Son meld together, merging in love.
And so here the Spirit flows, between the taut phallos
And the tremulous womb,
The male nerve and the female
Spirit moves and is one.

God not only loves us in and through our sexuality but, of course, delights in our own human lovemaking. That love of beauty, union, and creativity is the sexual drive itself and God's gift. Sexuality is an aspect of our deeply human yearning for fulfillment and meaning, for God. In its total pervasion of our lives, *eros* is the source of life and fuels all our loves—including our love for God!

Through our unique personalities we're called to shine back to God the joyful experience of loving and being loved sexually and spiritually. That response may be simply our daily amazement, wondering, yearning, expectation, and stunned delight at nature's wondrous bounty of dazzling color, scent, and sound—God's daily wooing of our hearts. We know the Beloved is near, indeed, resident within us always. We see his blood upon the rose, in the diamond eye and flashing wing of bluebird, while the white night awes our timid, quivering souls.

When we accept God's lovemaking, we grow even more, because now we become responsible for thinking through its meaning and for sharing that love with others. Faith comes by hearing. The fire in one heart ignites a like flame as we pass along the word: You are loved!

Each of us, operating on some theory of self and God, will through God's empowering love, deepen our understanding of ourselves as persons learning how to love. God, the greatest concentration of unitive energy in the universe, whose nature is love, loves us. Reaching beyond ourselves in a transcendent relationship with Her, we begin to accept Her love. Our love journey has begun, *we* are the beloved!

Paul, struggling to tell us about this miracle of oneness with God cried out, "No longer do I live, but Christ lives in me" (Galatians 2:20). He hadn't lost his identity by loving but had truly found it. Through the Spirit Paul was becoming like Christ and so lived in him. And that likeness, that identity, was a dynamic, personal transformation of power and love.

Identifying with Christ did not place Paul in some special unearthly atmosphere. Paul was talking about real union with a real person. When he said, "Have this mind in you which was also in Christ Jesus" (Philippians 2:5), he was speaking of modeling our behavior on the real, earthly acts of Christ in the Gospels. He was describing the likeness that resulted from the Spirit's living in him: "Reflecting as in a mirror the glory of the Lord, we are being transformed into his very image from glory to glory" (2 Corinthians 3:18). Impregnated with the Spirit's love, we too can give birth to love.

Paul's *agape* is a biblical way, then, to describe Toner's radical love and Moore's dynamic of falling in love. But Paul told us yet more: "Don't you know that your bodies are the temple of the Holy Spirit who is *in* you whom you have from God, and that you are not your own?" (1 Corinthians 6:19). He was speaking here of the Lover in the beloved as gift! That, we recognize, as the very nature of radical love itself.

For our learning how to live our love for one another, the idea of our bodies as God's living temples has tremendous importance, because we are also members one of another, deeply related through our embodied humanity, our common link with God our Lover. As God's condominiums, we house and nourish one another; sheltering and caring are part of our identity as men and women. Like parts of a body, we're called to cherish one another in every way, and to accept that cherishing. Daughters and sons of God, temples of the Spirit, how can we ever see another human as *enemy*? At the deepest level, each of us is a lover, with the saints members of God's household in the Body that is the People of God (Ephesians 2:19). Paul writes to the church as "one body and one spirit even as you are called in one hope of your calling; one Lord, one faith, one baptism, one God and father of all, who is above all, and throughout all, and in us all" (Ephesians 4:4-6).

Jerome Rausch in his study of *agape* and friendship, sees this oneness of ours in the Spirit as a unity in that love poured into us by God. Paul never analyzed that love, but described it knowing well that we must experience it, we must surrender to it, in order to understand it.

Recall the name that Jesus gave us at the Last Supper as our identity: "no longer servants, but friends" (John 15:15). We soon learn that friendship with one another is our major human task—and the highest we ever tackle. But friendship with God? How can we reach it? Dualism, the divine-human split, rears its ugly head again. How can we put together in love the human heart and God's? When we tell ourselves we're not worthy or capable of God's intimate friendship, we're just playing the same old poor-self- concept song! We are buying the split in the universe instead of listening to our own hearts. God says that our soul-scrubbing is just plain boring! How about listening to God's lovemaking instead? How about giving ourselves permission to be happy *because* God is in love with us? She keeps right on seducing us, so it's about time we took the hint. God is passionately, deeply serious about us; God is in love with us. We are the ones who can't trust that love, can't see that our weakness is God's opportunity to make us friends! Because that weakness is a capacity waiting to be filled—with God's loving, empowering cohabiting with us.

Literature and philosophy speak glowingly of friendship. Aristotle thought that the mark of real friendship is an honesty in which the friend is loved for himself/herself, and not for any good they might bring us. Later, when Thomas Aquinas developed a theory of Christian friendship, he qualified Aristotle's definition. According to Thomas, friendship has three conditions:

1. Friendship must be benevolent. Do I love you because you are useful to me or because you are rich or good at

sex? Or do I find you good in yourself and love you for yourself? If so, I love you with the love of *benevolence*; we are on the way to friendship.
2. Friendship supposes that the love is *mutual*. Not only do I try to love you, but my joy and good news is that you return my love. So now we have a common bond, a sharing of our lives, union; love has begun.
3. Friendship demands *communication* of this mutual, benevolent love. When this communion and sharing of ourselves takes place, we are loving each other as other selves.

Friendship to be real must exist in the hearts of the lovers themselves as love. Aquinas insists upon that relationship between love and friendship; he equates love *(amor)* and friendship; he calls human friendship love. He also applies his definition of friendship to charity, not only as love of God, but as a *"certain friendship"* with God! He implies a mutual return of love and a certain mutual community! Aquinas assumes that friendship with God is normal and expected. "Whoever abides in love, God abides in them, and they in God" (1 John 4:16). "God is faithful, to whom you have been called into fellowship with his son" (1 Corinthians 1:9).

Aquinas then asks, How is this sort of friendship with God possible while we live here embodied, mere earthlings? His answer can help us develop an embodied spirituality as our way to live this love of friendship with God. "But this society of man [and woman, I add] with God which is indeed a certain familiar conversation with God, is in fact begun here in this present life through grace; it is perfected in the future life."

The grace he speaks of is the *free* gift of God's own self to us, God's deepening always her life in our hearts. That familiar conversation with God begins only as we freely accept God's wooing, saying Yes to God's living within us as Lover. If our hearts move us to believe that God loves us and calls us to love in return, then we have begun right now a pattern of happiness, eternal life! We don't need to keep God in cold isolation any

longer, not this ardent Lover whose love is a burning fire, strong
as death and hard as hell, yet gentle as the evening breeze.

What does all this have to do with us as we humans try to
express love in intimate sexual form? Is sex a valid part of
human friendship? Many times it certainly is, a love full of
concern, self-sacrifice, caring, benevolence, wishing the other
every good. Sometimes, though, unreal sexual expectations
can turn an attempt to love into pain and frustration. Men have
hardly ever considered women their equals or thought women
capable of this real human friendship. But if women too are
God's lovers, capable of friendship with Him, why not with
God's image? (And surely men share that image with women.) If
both men and women accept our sexuality as a worthy way to
express love as mutual caring, we will see one another as equally
worthy of one another's and God's friendship; for our bodies
share in that image of God that we are.

Friendship, then, in its essence demands mutual caring in
love and a community of goods with a sharing of self, a familiar
conversation between equals. So, sexual love may frustrate us
when it is not an expression of friendship or cherishing with
equal regard or familiar conversation. Too often, it is familiarity
instead. Is it possible that our failure as men and women to
relate as friends has its roots still in this wounded self-image
we've discussed? Does it also come from our distorted images of
a God who is hardly a Lover?

> Certainly it is no wonder that most societies throughout
> history have looked with suspicion, derision, or active
> disapproval, on methods of education aimed at develop-
> ing individual freedom and the ability to love . . .
>
> Our own society seems to . . . allow freedom and
> love, but in a rather vague and hopeless way . . . What
> no culture has tried yet is a unified educational influence
> deliberately designed both to make love and freedom
> possible and to provide the supporting framework that can
> allow this to go on without social distress.
> —Rosemary Haughton

Let's turn now to consider radical love as the heart of sexual spirituality, healing that wounded self-image and transforming it into dynamic energy for a change of attitude, for the change of heart freeing us for a vital love life with human and divine lover.

4

Healing the Self-Image

Laura just would not respond! When we picked her up, her tiny body stiffened but no sound came. Day after day, we kept right on, hugging, kissing, fondling, caressing this poor little baby, her legs scarred from cigarette burns and bruises. This battered babe had, of course, been programmed not to cry. She was not to disturb her disturbed parents! But so wonderful is the resilience of human tissue that our loving finally won out. She cried! And soon she laughed. Love had done its healing thing.

Laura had learned that she was not worthy of expressing her needs; her damaged self-concept couldn't claim the right to express how she felt. Sexual spirituality is holistic (the Greek word *holos* is related to both "heal" and "whole"). It claims that right to express our real feelings. It tries to heal our images of self and God through love, just as love healed Laura. Healing always begins with the truth; denial is no approach to healing!

Who are we? And what does our self-image—the single most important component of how we act—look like today? W. H. Auden says, "The image of myself which I try to create in my own mind in order that I may love myself is very different from the image which I try to create in the minds of others so that they may love me." Auden pinpoints how we boost ourselves up inside, encouraging and supporting ourselves, and how we boost ourselves up in the presence of friends so that they'll accept us and approve of us. We communicate with self and others thus because we've been taught so to do, taught to think of ourselves a certain way.

How do you really feel about yourself? Are you at least as kind to yourself as you are to your friends? Too often, not; for some of us still carry inside the burden of a battered child, psychically and spiritually if not physically. Because children can feel great anger over their treatment by grownups, they

48

suffer guilt. "Good" children don't get angry at their "good" parents! So the cycle of anger and guilt rolls into depression and they are now "bad" children, so how can a bad child do good things? Confidence, the key to healthy self-image, slowly dies, and a pattern of distrust or even hatred of self is born. "I'm bad because I'm angry, so I'm not worth loving."

Even in persons who learn how to cope with home, school, and peers, that cycle of anger-guilt-depression can still be alive and well. It suddenly shows itself in inappropriate behavior that frightens or surprises us with our lack of control; but its roots lie in the unconscious, where we think we've so safely stowed it away. We can actually think of ourselves today as "good" professionals at our jobs but "bad" people, not a very empowering way to feel about ourselves! An anxious, neurotic approach to self provides little self-confidence or trust. How ever can we accept love when we are so unworthy? Especially, love from God, unconditioned and free?

A poor psychological image can also come from getting our self-worth from what we do, from our work. But we're not valuable because of what we *do*; we matter because of who we *are*, human persons loved by God, friends of Jesus, dignified receivers of love!

Believing this about ourselves can deliver us from another trap for the psychological self, getting our self-worth from pleasing others, a game we're taught from babyhood. Since work and approval can always change, getting our worth from them can leave us with no bedrock of support for our sense of our own value. In fact, basing it on other people's approval leaves us forever on the curb begging with our tin cup.

We also learn to value ourselves from adults vital to us— parents, teachers, and, later, friends. If they treat us with love and respect, as people with rights and needs, then we grow with confidence. If not, we learn to manipulate them to get our needs fulfilled. We conform to their needs, desires, and plans because of our naked need for approval, sometimes as strong as our need for food or shelter.

Approval is the meat of a child's psychological diet, so

children without it can actually die psychologically; they're just not buried. Parents' and teachers' expectations strangle the embryonic young thing, and the self that thinks, loves, falls, and rises again—the truly human self—never grows. Some of us have been battered as persons, but, like Laura, we are healable by that most powerful of healers, love.

Sometimes double damage occurs in the warping of the *sexual* self-image. The inflated expectations of society or family or church about how to be sexual so discourage us that in the real, sexual world we see spirituality as impossible for such "sinful" folk as us. Yet two ingredients of a good self-image, the psychological self and the bodily image, find their completion not in choosing spirit over sex but in that sexual spirituality that fuses both, because the person is both whole and holy and is loved into worthiness by God! Sexual spirituality means keeping it all together, body and spirit, because they're *already* one. From living in a self-hating society, we have absorbed through osmosis a world view that ignores that holiness of the body. Realizing, accepting, and using our oneness of spirit and body can ensure recovering that holiness.

One world view powerful until recently saw all of life operating under fixed, mechanistic laws. Our job then was to find them and obey them! Freud, Darwin, and even teachers of the spiritual life urged us to find and obey them in order to be wise or holy. That view meant that a "good" person was a law abider.

A holistic approach to sex, however, builds the self-image not by searching for fixed laws, but by involving our total self in many interacting areas whose rules change as situations change. Sexual, holistic spirituality takes the view that each situation and relationship must be dealt with individually, as we try to find the patterns, living our faith through real situations with real people. At the heart of the healing that sexual spirituality can bring is the truest, most "radical" love of all, God's love for us. This love can carry us through the crisis of trust or mistrust of life itself by telling us tha there *is* Somebody out there (and in here, too) who loves us unconditionally. And that love regularly revives us as we go through those crises on the road to full humanity. Accepting God's personal love for us carries us over the trust-mistrust crisis, the first psychosocial test, and lays the foundation of growth all through life, as we shall see when we look at changing our image of God. As we move toward a healed self-image, this learning to identify with God as faithful Lover will be crucial.

Still another area for love's healing activity is our image of our own bodies. How do we think of and picture ourselves as embodied? Put a pen in your right hand. Say to yourself, "I *have* a pen." That means you are also saying that you can be *without* it; for instance, you can drop it on the floor because it's separate from you.

Now pretend to hold your body in your hand and say, "I have a body." So it, too, is an object that can be divorced from you! A healthy self-image includes and incorporates the body, not as an object separate from us, but as a valid, equally dignified dimension of our humanness, a true part of our self. We *are* body-selves. So each of us can say, "I am embodied," with the emphasis on the "I." "I" names our person as the center of our doing, thinking, acting, and being. Embodiedness is another name for the self each of us is. Our bodies are not objects to be repressed, discarded, or despised, but a shining symbol of our self. Today we need to speak of enspirited bodiliness; too long we have concentrated on embodied spirits.

Our bodies can teach us about God, too, for as God's image they're part of the gift of God's meaning and message to us. Yet sexual bodiliness sometimes seems to spell spiritual trouble for some of us. Surely, some say, only a God with a sense of humor could have handed us the puzzle we seem to be! Yet we're told we are God's image. Does that mean only part of us, only our minds or spirits, and not our bodies? That's been the story. A sexual spirituality wants to change that for good—for *the body* as good! No spirituality is human unless it accepts the goodness and equal participation of the body in living out our faith.

The God who challenges us with the agony and ecstasy of living in bodies also happens to love us. Maybe we're not getting the message. Are we turned off by the difficulty of maturing? Are we afraid of that stretching tension of body, mind, and spirit?

In the Introduction we portrayed the negative bodily self-image formed from thinking of bodiliness as somehow evil or unclean. We lost the wonderful capacity to express spirit through body. Yet how else express it? What else did Shakespeare or Michelangelo or daVinci do? Sexual love and spirit were divorced. Yet it is love that makes us persons and true selves. The Christian put-down of the body expelled it from the spiritual life, so we were supposed to cultivate spirit alone in pursuit of God. Poor body was brother/sister ass, a prison house, or the devil's workshop!

Choosing today to relate to life in holistic fashion, we can no longer exile our bodies somewhere out there while we live our spiritual life in a dehumanized vacuum. Even today's science helps us see that there are no objects "out there," for we along with everything else are "showings forth" upon this earth of God's creative energy. As God's ideas we're one with the earth and the universe. Our bodies are our MasterCard in the human race, giving us free access to all the joy and pain of being human, equipping us for humanity's highest activity, love!

Living embodied spirituality calls to mind the prevailing public spirituality within which our See-Level is shaped, modern North American society. We can no longer image self or God without alluding to what Thomas Berry calls "the supreme historical event of modern times—the discovery of a new origin story about the universe as an emergent evolutionary process over some fifteen billion years." This discovery is of enormous significance because it can change how we will think about ourselves and God.

Yet, strangely enough, it's an event whose effects are neither well recognized nor well analyzed. It's a new story of the universe that will profoundly affect our picture of self and Creator, but, so far, science and theology do not address its meaning or evaluate it with any depth. A holistic spirituality must take into account this new picture of universe, self, and

God. Toward that enterprise, embodied spirituality is a small step.

Classic western spirituality not only malformed the image of person into a disembodied self, dividing it into sex and spirit; it eventually helped divide the divine and the human as well. God became transcendent, beyond everything and us, too. So we denied earth's deeply physical role as meeting place for God and us; even less could our bodies ever be that meeting place! We supposed over centuries that our humanity was somehow outside the world of nature, so nature became an object, too, even if we called it Mother Nature. Again, we divided nature, the divine, and the human.

Later thinkers even removed the life principle itself so that matter now became mere extension, lifeless, to be manipulated by us. Now, not only were body and spirit split, but we were cut off from nature, world, and God. No wonder western religions permitted the devastation of lands, forests, and waters—often in the name of progress and holy destiny for a nation. We had no responsibility for God's natural world because we had no kinship with it!

By recovering the holiness of the body as part of that natural world, we can develop a holistic approach to the body. Today we are involved in a process, an exciting historical reality in our religious time and tradition with its successes and failures. This transition time in thought and attitude is our chance to grow and change our world view.

Berry feels that we're called to the most significant change that western Christian spirituality has yet experienced, part of the larger change in human consciousness. The discovery of the evolutionary process, he feels, completes a 15-billion-year search for the universe's conscious reflection on itself and its development into human intelligence. The universe, like us, is changing, evolving—and thereby changing its self-consciousness, its self-image. So must we.

That's why there are no objects out there—like bodies! Rather than separate objects in the universe, we can know ourselves as *a way of being* in the earth's own process. We are not guests of, but a true part of, this earth, even if we seem its lords and ladies. Out of eons of development came our level of human consciousness, *the brain.* Equipped by nature to speak, we humans invented cultures with languages, customs, and spiritual values: brain, heart, and hand fashioned this, our world.

Out of that same development of some 4.5 billion years came, too, the human *body,* the *psyche,* and *spirit* in the last stage of the cosmic sequence. In the light of evolutionary theory, how can we ever again look down upon our bodies? They are nature's magnificent accomplishment, a vital part of God's world, ready at last to come into their own as worthy communicators of God's loving presence in the world!

This new world view signals the birth of a new theology and spirituality being born in this ecological age of oneness with the universe. The end of separateness will produce a holistic spirituality that gives the body its proper equal role as a sacrament of God's presence in the world, an outward sign of inward love. The characteristics of this spirituality, Berry feels, are revealed already by the earth itself as a message from God.

1. *Differentiation.* We are unique and historically irreplaceable in our proper personal role here. We have different See-Levels (addition mine).
2. *Subjectivity.* We humans are the maximum point of subjectivity, human consciousness.
3. *Communion.* We are related to all the universe in every way. Because we *are* one, we meet, drawn to one another, expressing love as the height of that communion. So also we can unite with God, the goal of any spirituality.

This communion is the lodestar of a sexual spirituality designed for friendship. If we're related to the whole universe, we restore the oneness of our bodiliness and the inhabiting spirit within us, since they equally emerge from the earth, the matrix of the human. That view highlights our crying need for a theology of *eros,* a theory of sexual love that accepts bodiliness as a valid part of holiness.

This earthy, holistic, sexual view of the body so emphasizes its dignity that it can help to heal our self-image and show us a sensuous, healthy way to live our faith in God's love in Christ here and now. That view can also heal the myths of separation of body and soul, and, so, of universe, human, and God. Living this individually can help transform, too, our culture's present view of embodiedness:

> Sex is a torment, a possession, a weapon against the world. . . . Gratitude for sexuality as enrichment of life, for ecstatic joy, and serenity of faithful companionship— all this gets left out of the meaning of sex.
> —Daniel Day Williams

A new way to look at self will mean a new way to see our ensexed bodies. Sexuality becomes a pervasive aspect of our personhood affecting our feelings and acts. It will include our body-self, making us one in all dimensions as a symbol of our need to communicate with others also one with us. We are made for relationship, so sexuality is also essential to our relationship to God, not incidental to it. It calls us to practice more and more fully our power of relating in love to others, our most valid way to love God. At its most profound level, then, sexuality will be the longing for and the expression of union with others as body-selves and with God's self as well.

A new way, a new theory or theology of sexual love, will mean starting with accepting yourself as somebody loved by God, a God who accepts you totally, including your body and its sexual drives for oneness and communion. She accepts you when you experience your selfishness and the sexual fantasies that arise from being human, whether you be hetero/homo/bisexual, whether male or female, whether prayerful or confused or lost or not concerned with keeping in touch with God about sex right now. That theology of God's unconditioned love applies to the total you—bodiliness and sexuality included! No wonder the Christian story of God is called Good News!

The mystics experienced their male or female sexuality, too, as they encountered God in contemplative union. The body is our way, as it was theirs, to come into this world as trysting place for making love with both God and human lover. In our body-selves God delights; we are God's pleasure palace. God's delight is to be with us; so we thank God for our sexual selves, we don't mourn over them. God, not the devil, designed our bodies as beautiful images of who She is: *the* tremendous Lover! Our bodies are sacraments of God's need and our need to communicate, to reach out to others in caring, concern, love, giving and receiving our healing.

Even when we stupidly drive them with our compulsive minds, our bodies can stubbornly remind us of their true purpose, their glorious meaning: to move toward oneness. Jesus, as prime Word of God, says in his very person who God is and shows in all his attitudes and actions his Father's being, which is love. "When we meet God's love in the love of Jesus we don't meet *agape*, or selfless love as different from *eros*. . . . Rather, it is to encounter a distinct form of erotic attraction" (Martin Buber).

That is not exactly the usual way some theologies see Jesus; rather, he seems to be deprived of sexuality. A desexed Jesus is also part of the distrust of the body in some Christian spiritualities.

Living in an age of free sexual expression like ours, we might feel that embodiedness is accepted as healthy. But the cult of the body beautiful, that never aging creation of the advertising media, is a sign of disease for both men and women. Forced by our culture to be forever young, how can we face the reality of bodies that grow old and sick? Our culture denies the fact that bodies change, age, die; the denial of death is part of a youth-worshiping culture in which one must never grow old. Do we ever see a *celebration* of the "end of living" outside of some liturgies of some churches? In a changing world always in process, our bodies' aging and transitions are normal—not fearful, disgraceful events to be hidden and avoided at all costs. Death, though we may be conditioned to fear it, is part of our story, our personal process—an ecologically sound transition to another phase of living.

Our sensual age *professes* to worship the body, particularly woman's, but it actually despises and rejects its truth. We hate the fact that the body adamantly refuses to live up to the advertising, to the expectations of the media: We should not die; we should neither age nor wither; we must scramble hopelessly to preserve the appearance of youth. We're urged to practice dishonesty in ways that can hinder the healing of our self-image. A friend of mine spent a year in the heart of Africa—no full-length mirror, no television. She said that gradually she grew less and less worried about how she looked (no media were telling her how to look!). She started to value herself more and more and stopped worrying about what other people thought of her clothes, hair, skin, makeup. She said it was the freest, most contented year of her life.

The Older Women's League (OWL), centered in Washington, D.C., a brave attempt to fight the cultural pressure to be forever young, invites women of middle and upper years to claim their *right to age*, to come out of the closet! If Cary Grant can do it, why not women? Their anti-cultural thrust may herald a breakthrough in *real* feminist liberation: freedom from tyrannical expectations laid on women to look like the ads, to pant after an under-thirty look, to keep on lying about their looks, as they're so often pressured to lie about their feelings. The League's attitude and practice is a healthy approach to the ever changing process that bodiliness is; it frees us to be human, changing creatures of a day, ephemeral, yes; but, also, permanent residents of the larger realm, God's total universe, in which we continue after this earthly phase.

Charles Davis would call "sensual" that pursuit of the will-o'-the-wisp of youth, for it rejects the real body. Instead it lashes the body against its own better wisdom and drives it to obey the compulsive mind's egocentric foolishness.

In their attempt to express love as caring, both the mystic and the sexual lover learn to enjoy the body as God's pleasure palace, using the sensuous mode, delighting with one's lover in the joyful play of the senses. Both their experiences can go to the

heart of reality—listening, open, holding oneself lovingly
aware of the other, willing to surrender in the giving and
receiving of body, mind, and heart. This loving builds the self-
concept, in contrast to the tyranny of "forever young," which
cannot help but disappoint us and ultimately destroy the self-
concept.

Paradoxically, as Davis sees it, both the puritan and the
libertine are guilty of sensuality, a compulsive idolizing of the
body, but for different reasons. The puritan wants to get rid of
the body as an obstacle to the spiritual life; the libertine uses it as
a tool for pleasure. So both reject bodiliness itself, fearing its
spontaneous sexual drive. They ignore its holiness and symbolic meaning as a sign of the indwelling Spirit. Both reduce it
to an object, putting it in opposition to mind and reason. Both
shut themselves off from feeling as a response to value. Both sin
against bodiliness as gift of God. Finally, both idolize sexuality
instead of seeing it as only one natural enjoyable part of human
personality. So, keeping the body in a box, they keep it out of
authentic touch with the self, so the price is high. When we
suppress powerful energies like sexuality, they have a way of
rebelling in rage. Then they really do become "unspiritual."
When we treat the body as some distrusted, somehow disgraceful, alienated thing, it protests in sickness, psychotic disor-
ders, or spiritual trauma.

Yet when we embrace with honesty the fact that, like the
trees about us, we change, age, and die, we *can* live the
"sensuous" life: We permit feeling in all of life's experiences,
mental and spiritual as well as bodily; we do not confine strong
emotion to the few moments of sexual intercourse; we allow the
body spontaneously to feel, react, and respond to healthy
stimuli!

No wonder psychiatrists' couches are full! Society's (and
Christianity's) expectations make sexuality one minute good—
marriage; and the next minute bad—extramarital intercourse;
now approved, now disapproved! And all the time the body—
not those mixed messages from parent, church, or society—is
the whipping boy/girl.

The puritan ends up in depression or guilt, while the libertine finally surrenders to boredom. So much for sex as the god-in-the-box. When we see sex as *one dimension* of ourselves, one way to express caring and concern, we can enjoy it as it is, rather than as we've been socialized to see it. Alan Watts poses the problem thus:

> To the degree that we do not yet know what man [sic] is, we do not yet know what human sexuality is. We do not know what man is so long as we know them piecemeal, categorically, as the separate individual, the agglomeration of blocklike instincts and passions and sensations regarded one by one under the fixed-stare of an exclusive consciousness.
>
> What we are and what human sexuality is will come to be known as we lay ourselves open to experience the full sensitivity of feeling which does not grasp.

We sometimes hear attitudes about bodiliness like "How odd of God to make the bod'." But I believe the Designer had it together when She provided us with the equipment called sex and spirit in embodied form. Our attitudes must sometimes disappoint the Designer! Instead of the applause She expected when the model was first unveiled came stares of disbelief, even charges of indecency! Some religions didn't welcome the ensexed, embodied model too warmly. People feared and were suspicious of the body's power to erupt sexually and break through reason's controls. So they devised theories about how to handle the total package, for example, Christianity's dualism, the mind-body split. No religion we know of ever declared the body inherently evil, yet moral laws and religious practice often implied it.

As the joyful meeting place of sex and spirit, the body is defended by John Milhaven. He cites three things we all yearn for that embodiedness provides:

1. In sex, we are able to feel, come alive, and experience the joy of strong feeling.

2. We feel absorbing pleasure, and let our whole consciousness, our whole self go, and identify with pleasure because we feel securely loved.
3. We become open to each other; we become one in the
   overflowing feelings of ourselves. Breaking out of our
   shells, we share our joy and satisfaction.

Milhaven emphasizes the celebration of bodiliness, of joy in
play and oneness of spirit, just for the fun of it. "Having fun can
be one of the finest, deepest, most personal ways of humans
being together. And this without thinking about it!" Such
thinking can heal the self-concept because we can then
embrace our embodiedness and celebrate living and loving
through the body's play, meaning, and relationship. The body
then has the same goals as spirit: to express love through union.
Prayer, religious experience, and works—all of them are sterile
and not spiritual at all if they don't fulfill the highest human
goal: to receive and express love. The body is sensuously
delighted in the expression of love, as are the mind and spirit.
Never again can we divorce our bodiliness from our spiritual
living.

If we begin to identify with our bodies in this sensuous,
joyful, loving, responsible way, we change our self-concept.
Further, all the powers, joys, and sorrows of bodiliness help
create the very stages of the spiritual life itself. "We create the so-
called 'Interior Life' by our loving responses to God and each
other—or we are dead within," says Thomas Merton. Accepting the body increases the joy of the total self; we have so many
avenues to feel everything life sends— sunsets, bird songs, love
looks, gentle touches, delightful fragrance—all of them sing
God's love song in our hearts: "You are mine; you are loved."

A final reason for embracing embodiment and sexuality as
powerful aids for the spiritual self-image is the miracle we
mentioned earlier, the human brain—perhaps the most exciting area of research for the 80s. Behavioral and cognitive
psychologists are studying both how the brain responds to the
world in sexual difference and how the world brings data to the

brain, whether sensuous, psychic, and spiritual.

In a world where all is emerging, the brain as end product of that evolution holds yet untapped secrets about our sexuality. Researchers now wonder how much the brain, as conductor of the body's hormones (including sex hormones) is also influenced by them, even how much the brain, too, is "ensexed." The hypothalmus, as differently sexed, controls the flow of hormones and is somehow stamped before birth by them. This view puts the brain back into the body as an integral, *material* part, not some ivory tower where mighty reason reigns alone. Restoring the brain as part of the sexual life integrates the total body. The brain's wonders certainly can enhance our respect for our bodies, shore up our self-concept, and restore the body as an honorable vehicle for spiritual power.

The brain's branches laid end to end would stretch to the moon and back. This forest of 100 billion nerve cells in its bony skull-cage actually *is* who we are, for the roots of all our acts and skills lie in the brain. Research produces yet more respect for "matter" as alive, for we now know that the brain is also a gland, a thinking, dreaming sex gland! So where now is that famed superiority of pure, non material reason over that wretched bodiliness whose agent is our splendid brain? But even more is yet to come, for we today know about as much about the brain as we did about physics before the discovery of electricity. Yet these marvelous powers of ours operate constantly, affecting our feelings, thoughts, decisions, and motivations. Certainly, the brain, along with so-called spiritual powers, does affect how we live our faith as well. Research may some day even help us know how God operates in our bodies, psyches, and spirits, for these are only words for functions of the one self, his beloved.

What magnificent beings we are! We embodied humans crown God's creation. It is difficult then to continue to cherish a low self-concept based on a low estimate of our bodies as troublemakers.

Contemporary psychiatry is teaching us that trust in one's body is essential to personal health. . . . The body will

destroy the facades that people erect to hide their true
selves from themselves and from the world. But it will also
open a new depth of being and add a richness to life
compared to which the wealth of the world is a mere trifle.
                                        —Alexander Lowen

These ideas will upgrade the body's image. But real growth in
our self-esteem comes not from awareness of our marvelous
brains, keen minds, and beautiful bodies, or because of what we
do or don't do, but because we know we are God's image,
human persons, dignified as God's beloved on this earth.
Therapists can help us accept what we may not have had in
childhood—love, respect, and trust—to rebuild our self-image.
Drugs may cheer us up or calm us down. Friends may reassure
us of our worth. But we need something more.

Carl Jung concluded that psychological problems in those
over thirty-five were basically religious problems related to *false
images of God*. The same applies to those of us with a poor self-
concept. Too often we have an image of God as someone with a
long white beard, floating somewhere on a cloud recording on
his computer our every peccadillo.

The deepest healing of our immature, warped images of
God and self will come from the total acceptance of God's love.
Our spirituality, after all, acts out how we image and respond to
God; if a poor image of our bodies can lead to low esteem, so
also the way we imagine God may keep us from thinking well of
ourselves. Still more, keep us from ever aspiring to intimate
friendship with a God who can never relate to our sexuality—
even though He invented it! Perhaps deep within us we have an
image of God that alienates us from Him.

Scientific research will indeed increase our esteem for our
bodies, but the greatest growth in self-concept will come from
accepting God's radical love, the greatest intensity of love in all
of creation, and from knowing that it is ours for the accepting!

To get at the core of God at his greatest, one must first get
into the core of himself at his least, for no one can know
God who has not first known himself. Go to the depths of

the soul, the secret place of the Most High, to the roots, to
the heights; for all that God can do is focused there.
                                              —Meister Eckhart

5

Who Is Your God?

We do not need God in order that he may teach us the truth of things, or the beauty of them . . . but in order that he may save us, in order that he may not let us die utterly.

—Miguel de Unamuno

"Yell at God? Don't you think I'm in enough trouble already? That's exactly why I don't pray. I'm afraid, guilty, angry! So how can I talk to God? Yelling at God won't help our relationship!" Norma Rae's eyes filled with tears as she pushed my idea away.

"Norma, that's exactly why we yell." I reached for her hand and held it hard. "God's no computer in the sky but someone who loves us incredibly. God doesn't care a bit about our yelling; She loves it! It means we think She's real. We wouldn't yell if we didn't believe She could hear us. And remember I mean really yell—in the car where we could die and nobody would hear us. Open up that ribcage and feel the anger tearing up your throat and onto your tongue. God wants to hear from the heart and that's where those powerful feelings come from. Give it a try."

I've heard Norma's story over and over again wherever people share frustrations about not being able to pray or even to turn to God for help. We feel too unworthy. We have messed up our lives too much to speak to the spotless, timeless, unchanging (unfeeling), all-powerful, all-knowing (disapproving!) someone called God, the bizarre product of centuries of destructive images. So let's remove them!

The first obstacle to letting God love us sexually as well as spiritually is a possibly damaged view of our own bodies and their sexual powers. We may really fear our own sexuality as a source of pain, anger, and guilt. Guilt may lessen if we also replace an asexual, uninvolved God with the God who wants to share our real struggles. A nonsexual, disembodied God is only the logical outcome of centuries of refusing equal status to the body in the spiritual life.

Any statement about God is a statement about ourselves. What else do we have as a basis of comparison but our own human experiences? Yet, amazingly enough, Christian theologies about God abound, theologies that talk as if we really *knew* who God is, as if our theories are adequate and complete, even verifiable! But then theology is that brave science that studies that mystery called God, yet talks as if it knew exactly what it was talking about.

Statements about us are also somehow statements about God. But we have next to nothing in such theologies about how our sexuality and embodiedness relate to and are one with our spirituality. We have volumes about what we know least, God, and mere pamphlets about what we want so much to understand, our experience of sexuality and our struggles to comprehend its meaning in living our faith.

Over centuries we seemed to have neither time nor energy to study how the human person operates. Which of us really knows what we are? Irenaeus said that the glory of God is the human person fully alive. But that insight somehow got lost in the shuffle. We had wars to fight and power to guard, so we still know little about the human person and our sexual, psychic, or spiritual powers.

That emphasis on studying God, though, was a normal human development because theories about God multiplied in periods when certain questions about the meaning of our lives became crucial. So God was a question all the time, and theologians and philosophers struggled with theories about Him. Yet eventually some theories about God turned God right out of his world; soon they said that the human had little to do with the divine, or God with the material world. So here we are today with images of a God divorced from us. Of course we feel alienated and alone.

The Reformation produced a Protestant emphasis on a

transcendent God beyond us—absolute, changeless, un-created, an independent reality. A necessary correction for the time, it still led to denying our experience of an immanent God *within*, attracting us and yearning to be our Friend.

In early Christianity believers called Christ God and Redeemer, and soon the doctrine of the Trinity, one God in three persons, sprang from their need to account for the religious facts of Christianity. In fact, Athenagoras defined Christians as "men who hold the Father to be God, the Son of God, and the Spirit Holy." But these were not to him just names for God; they were individual substantive objects. How did one image that?

Not until the mid-fourth century did theologians state the independence of the three persons in God and their oneness in being. One in content and consciousness, but three to contact and apprehension. Heresies came and went, and Athanasius saved Christian monotheism, the theory of the "identity of substance" in God.

Finally theologians concluded that in God's life there exists only one function of will and one principle of action. Three persons were not to be regarded as three independent con-sciousnesses. So, theologies struggled to express the meaning of the faith-experience of early Christians. What did it mean to love God? Who was She or He?

We've been conditioned to think of ourselves as not responsi-ble for theologizing, but at the Council of Ephesus (431 A.D.) the streets rang with the cries of street corner theologians, vendors and buyers, shouting the name of a woman: "Mary is Mother of God." And the grave fathers of the Council responded by defining that she was such to save belief in the Incarnation, the becoming human of Jesus the Christ. They said "one nature (it meant 'person' then), incarnate of the Son of God." God's image was evolving again. And more closely connected with humans; he had a real woman for his mother. A closer bond? Yes and no, as we shall see. It became necessary to dehumanize Mary somewhat to please the antisexual, anti-body tradition.

Fuzziness about the meaning of Christ's nature finally led to a compromise between two great theologians, John of Antioch and Cyril of Alexandria. "Jesus was one in substance with his Father; one in substance with us in his humanity." Incarnation was clearly stated so we had someone to identify with. Jesus Christ was God and human, according to their description.

Out of the fifth century came the Neoplatonist, Denis the Areopagite, whose writing had an enormous influence on our idea of God. He taught a hierarchical universe coming down from a God above, moving through higher spirits to the lower realms of creation. We can, he said, ascend to the vision of God through ecstasy, thus adding a mystical nuance to the God image that pervaded all of Greek theology. Through Western medieval writers that kind of God came to our time.

While in the West writers like Augustine struggled over our perennial questions—What is the human person? How are humans free?—the Eastern Fathers worked out theories about the nature of Christ. This story of the struggle by early theologians for meaning may help us today to discard any negative images of God we might have inherited from those theological battles, especially whatever alienates us from God.

Yet it's reassuring to see our goal of accepting the holiness of our bodies confirmed by these theological gymnastics seeking to preserve bodily humanity. The real *embodiedness* of Jesus, they said, was neither an appearance nor a phantom, but flesh and blood like ours. Battles were fought in the streets; bishops were imprisoned, exiled, even killed over these questions about God and Christ. Theology is theory about God, but the struggle of the theologians was so long and painful that their answers, once they had been finalized, seemed written in concrete and were passed on as such.

So when we think of God today, behind us stretches a long trail of 2,000 years of Christians pondering, searching, seeking *somewhat adequate* images of God, and ways to think about Her. Actually there is no thought, but only thinkers who see the world and God through those images fed into their different See-Levels and who have trouble seeing it through anyone else's.

Later Western theologians had only those early theologians' decisions about God, plus the writings of Augustine, as materials for their search. As the "barbarian" invasions swept away ancient sees like Antioch and Constantinople and the Moslems closed off from the West the Greek churches and their theology, medieval western Europe lost the ability to read Greek and, so, lost Greek theology. So ways to think of God were limited by geography for a long time.

Today's images of God have their roots not only in the later recovery of Greek theology, but also in the inferior theology handbooks of the fifth to seventh centuries, when Christians strove to handle in ever poorer Latin the old arguments of the great theoreticians before them. Decadent theology had arrived. Few Western writers felt called to rethink how we are divinized (made like God), an idea in seed in the New Testament. The question of our relationship to God, so vital to Athanasius and to Gregory of Nyssa, the founder of spiritual theology, was neglected in the struggle for physical survival.

Today's theology, influenced like that of the early church by political, scientific, and cultural changes, images God from that long story, but breaks through—as it must—to rethink God in our terms and times. New concepts of an evolving universe demand new images of God. Our knowledge of the function of language, for instance, helps us understand that the word God is a symbol for the reality of God, so it can no longer be described solely in masculine images or words; God cannot be confined to one sexual category.

Some biblical scholars even suggest that Jesus spoke of God as Father not in order to totally describe God but to provide a new image of God for his day to counteract the Old Testament emphasis on God as King. Others feel that Christ manifested an androgynous personality in the Gospels.

We can look to medieval spirituality for other descriptions of God, such as feminine images. Anselm of Canterbury called Jesus "Our Mother," like the mother hen in the New Testament (Matthew 23:37). Julian of Norwich calls Christ the "Mother suckling our souls." Many of us, fed theologies from books or from Bible study tidbits, have suffered from ignorance of these feminine Christian images in our history. Seldom have we been challenged to theologize for *ourselves*, examine *our* images, or learn to express *our own* experience of God's Spirit. We were not taught to value our faith experience as precious data for theological reflection, nor to ask what our experience meant.

Throughout this book I have, therefore, purposely used different genders for God, not because I know God is either masculine, feminine, or both, but to jog possibly "stuck" images of God in our minds. We don't know that God is without sexuality either, so again I have given male and female equal time, letting the written word testify both to God's transcending and yet somehow including sexuality in God's life.

In this connection, Professor Jeanne Block's terms "agency" and "communion" for what we have always called "masculine" and "feminine" make sense. God may be androgynous, combining the best of both these qualities; God may be neither. But if we are made in God's image, our undying desire for communicating, for meaning, and for union must mirror something somehow of God's inner love life, call that what we may.

The concreteness that confines God to our assumed likeness leads us to play God. So thinking of God as other than masculine actually releases us from a static God image inside. Refusing to see God in different ways or to accept the challenge to change images could even delay the call to mature as ensexed lovers of God.

If God has for us that radical love we discussed earlier, then this God shares our very lives through that burning love. Doesn't this kind of God project a fresh image? We too, then, can experience God's very life as our own. Can we possibly entertain and learn to live with this ardent image of God as Lover?

If we *stay open* to letting God be whatever God is, some part of ourselves learns to surrender in love to this God—whether body, mind, or spirit—and thus mystical union begins. By this letting go to God in love, we're not demeaned but dignified, not lessened but fulfilled, because of the dignity of God, our Beloved. We too can give God something God lacks and wants, our love.

This idea of a sexual, even androgynous God may shake free images that have kept us from picturing God as someone who loves us passionately and is deeply involved with us. God is always communicating and relating in familiar conversation with us. Gone is the God in the icebox. Here is the God with a passion for us.

False images of a distant God came also from fear of the body's own passion that one could never bring to God in prayer. They also came from absence of women among those who explained what it means to be Christian and to love God. These two situations gave birth to a distorted image of a God cerebral and solely male. Certainly He was not seen as tender Lover, surely not as intimate Friend.

Changing our image of God to faithful Lover gives us a new image of the body as good, as God's very temple and the sacred space of our meeting with God. That new image can come, too, from the newly valued presence of woman in church and society, coequal with man as lover of God upon earth.

This new picture of God as susceptible and responsible Lover yearning for our response to his love also strongly affects fears we may have about our mortal destiny. It delivers us from the fear of death and gives us a different way to look at our own. The word *death* itself appears a misnomer in the light of a Lover-God who is gift, friend, and cosufferer.

Peter Berger says that the power of religion can be judged by the banners (the courage) it can place in our hands in the face of death. Christians can find a fresh meaning in the resurrection of the body and life after death if we adjust lenses to see God as a living part of that adventure we call death. Personal survival after death makes more sense if we see God as a *continuing* part of our experience. For it is our relationship with God as Friend and Lover that makes life after death a reunion banquet devoutly to be wished, a coming home to the Beloved.

How important it is, then, to start discarding childish images of God and shaping mature ones to fit our adult experiences of loving! The goal of all valid theologies is meaning. Our beliefs are not things to be proved, but ideas to interpret our human experience so we have that meaning.

Still, no matter how we answer the question of our meaning, death seems to end all the loving relationships that make us human. We're afraid, not just that they must end, but that we will end with them. Eugene Fontinell says, "Everything depends upon whether one of the relations here and now that makes us person is with another personal center—one having the quality of transcendence." This transcendent center (God) must have power to maintain both the relationship and us when we no longer relate to time. God as Lover longs, too, to maintain the relationship, and *does*.

Another reason to adjust our images of God and self comes from the idea of "person" as a *complex of "fields"* discussed above. William James' comment applies: "Whatever else is certain, this at least is—that the world of our present knowledge is enveloped in a larger world of some sort of whose residual properties we at present can frame no positive idea." We have traditionally called that *wider field* "God." And seeing that God as a Lover assures us of Her longing to continue the relationship beyond death.

A final approach to fresh images of God that support a sexual spirituality comes from the East, as Thomas Merton discovered. Buddhist thinkers address both our questions: Who are we humans? Who is God? Their insights cannot be ignored in the (hoped-for) united world of East and West that ecumenical action can fuse if we wish to save our planet and begin anew. We can find help from Buddhist experience in changing our God images and clarifying our love place in this sexual-spiritual world.

Valuable indeed is the Buddhist reminder that a deep experience of God is not dualistic, not split into mind and body; beneath the experience of the individual self is an immediate experience of being. It is not consciousness of something, but pure consciousness in which the subject as such disappears.

Thomas Merton says the distinction between Creator and creature does not preclude a unity within ourselves at the peak of our being where we and the world are one with God. His theology takes into account an emerging universe in process, making God and the world neither one nor two, but with their being in each other; the *true self* of the human is the life of God within us.

This idea lets God be a God of this world, acting in history, really embodied not only in Jesus but in all of nature and in us, and so redeeming the bodily stuff of the earth. Even more exciting is some Buddhist thought on the puzzle of human nature. It sees the deepest self as no self, meaning that to be seized by God's love is to know that our true selves are divine selves. The idea of no self doesn't cut us off from God. We're distinct from him and yet identified through love and freedom to be but "one self," in Merton's words. He means that the transcendent self is our *true self.*

Now no longer separated from God we realize that in our deepest being "his presence is present in my own presence." Augustine said it, too, long ago; God is to us *intimior intimo meo,* more intimate than my most intimate self. Merton feels that this experience of grace, realizing ourselves as no self, makes sense of biblical Christian images like Paul's, "I live now, not I, but Christ lives in me" (Galatians 2:20).

This image of God as Lover is relevant because, made one with the divine self, we find our love identified with Love itself, not two loves now, but Love, loving in freedom. Merton's appropriation of Buddhist insights also helps overcome the dualism we saw as a chief enemy of a healthy self-concept. It restores bodiliness as worthy partner with spirit in the total human-divine relationship.

Now we can think of God as our truest self whose nature it is to love. God, living her life in us, must communicate; such is her nature. So this Lover God actually rejoices in her need for us so that *She* can be her true self, our Lover! This does not limit God, but fulfills Her. We thrill at being part of God's joy and are awed at our new image of friendship, cooperation, and coresponsibility with God for changing the world.

This new image can lead to a deeper meaning of what "sin" might be in such a context of love and friendship. Rather than an endless listing of sexual failures, real sin now appears as that blinded imaging of ourselves and God as *separate*, that ancient enemy dualism once again. Separation is actually a false consciousness, making God, self, and the world into individual existences. This false consciousness harbors a false image of God that can be transformed by what Paul saw as putting on the mind of Christ (c.f. Galatians 2:20).

We here assume, like so many before us struggling with the problem of evil, that sin is curable ignorance, with the result that on this earth we ourselves must have an integral part in that healing. This theory, a hopeful attitude, helps foster a holistic spirituality that embraces sexuality as vital energy for spiritual living. It has profound results in enlarging responsibility for working with God and neighbor for a renewed earth, the kingdom of God in this world. Merton found that kingdom to be both present and future:

> Christianity moves in an essentially historical dimension toward the restoration of all things in Christ. Yet with Christ's conquest of death and the sending of the Holy Spirit that restoration has already been accomplished. What remains is for it to be made manifest.

What a thrilling image of God Merton here implies! This world, our mutual home with God, is God's cosmic dance. "Hear his call and follow Him in his mysterious cosmic dance knowing that . . . no despair of ours can alter the reality of things or stain the joy of the cosmic-dance which is always there."

Paul Knitter's study of Merton reveals an image of God willing to do and be what He is through our actions. As we move toward using God's sexual spiritual energy, we can never forget our neighbor's need for food, housing, education, love, joy. All of these God wants for them, but through us, through one another; this is the actualizing, the real putting on the mind of

Christ.

We Christians are called to be Christ loving now in and through us. "Our life in this world is his life lived in us." This is our deepest meaning: cohealers with God of our world. Grounding our work in the world in contemplative union with God through prayer provides a safeguard against burnout from overactivism. Each of us, praying our own way, joins the cosmic dance as God teaches the steps, ever more intricate, ever more delightful. The work, then, is there for us; we are not there solely for the work, no matter what we've been taught! Sometimes we sit one out; we contemplate. Sometimes we lead. Sometimes we follow. As God's lovers, we're always prior *as person* to any work of ministering or serving. Yet the work can be the magic trysting place of God, neighbor, and ourselves, the present and future kingdom. That view of ourselves as coworkers with God can keep us from wanting to wipe out opponents or competition and from failing to accept difference or to respect disagreement. (Disagreement itself can be a form of love as honesty.)

Coaction with God and neighbor gives us a new vision of ourselves, a healed self-image: We matter! And this new vision affects that other desired healing, our picture of God within. We also matter to God. God as our truest self can never again be our prison guard. This God's love embraces every tribe, tongue, color, rank, and sex. This God is a universal God whose name is "Faithful," yet one who can love us individually. He calls no one "stranger." So how can we?

A fresh God image delivers us from the fear of death, then; it energizes us to accept the good news: We are loved, and forever! So we take life day by day lightly, trusting this God. We are thus energized for concern for others, too, yet delivered from playing Messiah. We know that God's power is available to us if only we go with the river and stop scrubbing the raft. If we let go and let God be whoever God wants to be to us.

One last point about imaging God. Our See-Level may suffer a "C.B.," a cultural bump of fear or shock, if we think of God as somehow sexual—perhaps a natural reaction from our split-level, dualist past. Yet we're told that God created us male and female in God's image (Genesis 1:27). Perhaps the writer uses the myth to help us see what we have lost. Yet it seems to me that male and female sexual embodiedness (and its expression in erotic love) must mirror God's being in some way.

The need for completion is probably part of God's sexuality as well as ours. A God with sexuality as capacity for union must be geared for relationships, must desire communion. Such a God can never, ever stop being "person," which means God is open to meaning somehow like our own. For being a person embodied means precisely being open to the relationships that follow from embodiment. God as love would, then, have infinite openness to *all* meaning, including ours, and to the relationships that must follow. Our mutual love (God and us) both divinizes us and completes our humanity and God's being God.

We're also told that Jesus Christ became human, took on flesh, was embodied, and was ensexed as we are. Jesus was a sexual human being. Sexual love is a human way of knowing and loving, but we somehow exclude Jesus from that experience of his own human sexuality. We seem afraid to let him enjoy truly sensuous, embodied use of the gift of sexuality, even of genitality. If body is good, if human sexuality is gift, that attitude needs changing.

In former theology of "omission" both God and body were allegorized away. We were God's image, but not in our bodies! The likeliness of God had to be in our souls! We were taught that we pleased God more by denying bodiliness and promoting spirit as the more perfect way to be human. God became thus an unfeeling, male, celibate God. What a surprise that must have been to God, the dynamic source of the love energy of the universe, the God of the cosmic love dance in whom the fire and the rose are one!

The mystery of human sexuality must have deep meaning, for God does not make jokes about us, so we are superbly equipped for relationship. We, of course, do not know how God is sexual; but if we have the joy of sensuous relationship and

experience, surely God has no less. Even if we don't understand
how God relates within God's love life, may we not presume
that God, too, as lover, has organs of relationship? God not only
is love, God makes love, as all the mystics can testify. God then
must also relate passionately to God in love even if we understand not the how of it. After all, that's what heaven's for.

Someone has said that the Holy Spirit is God's passion for
God. I wonder if the Spirit is not also God's self-image, like
ours, the most important component of God's activity called
love? God thinks of self and the flame of love bursts forth: the
Spirit! Jesus said. "I have come to light a fire on the earth, and
how I wish it were already kindled!" (Luke 12:49). The Spirit
came when Jesus left us and that same Spirit enflames our
hearts with love at this moment.

God who made us for love surely makes love. God must be
possessed of divine means of relating intimately, means perhaps
somehow like our own. I'm sure that God, the source of all
delight, whose being is love, is not disturbed by our fumbling
attempts to understand the divine love life. For if God is
anyone, God is the Lover we see dramatically portrayed in the
works of the mystics, those passionate lovers of God.

When God makes love, they tell us, it can involve bodily
rapture, a delightful inebriation, an intercourse with divine
love. Teresa of Avila speaks of the soul willing to be in

the paradise of delights, made one with the Lord of
love. . . . Nor can one merit so delightful a favor from
the Lord, so intimate a union or a love so destined to be
experienced and felt. . . . Grant me this favor: Let Him
kiss me with the kiss of His mouth, for without You, what
am I, Lord? Now, I see, my Bridegroom, that You are
mine!

Hadewijch, a Beguine mystic of the thirteenth century, says
that

the soul is a bottomless abyss in which God suffices to
himself; and his own self-sufficiency ever finds fruition in

this soul to the full, as the soul, for its part, ever does in him. Soul is a way for the passage of God from his depths into his liberty; and God is a way for the passage of the soul into its liberty . . . into his inmost depths, which cannot be touched except by the soul's abyss. . . . So long as God doesn't belong to her in his totality, he doesn't truly satisfy her.

In perhaps the most famous of all mystical poems, John of the Cross speaks of the heavenly Lover.

When the breeze blew from the turret
Parting His hair,
He wounded my neck
With his gentle hand
Suspending all my senses.

I abandoned and forgot myself
Laying my face on my Beloved;
All things ceased; I went out from myself,
Leaving my cares
    Forgotten among the lilies.

True mystics receive the freedom of the children of God in their bodies as well as in their spirits, for bodies, too, are the rendezvous, the trysting place of God, their truest self. Michel de Certeau quotes a medieval monk: "The sensible is the cause of the conceptual; the body is the cause of the soul and precedes it in the intellect." The body held erect in prayer, the hands to the heavens, was called the language of desire. Like "a tree in the night, without it being necessary to add the sound of words," the soul held deepest intercourse with God.

God loves us sexually because God loves us always appropriately, and we are humans. Embodiedness becomes the magic ring, the sacred space for the act of worship that union with God means. In that act of love God burns away the dross, and the soul is afire with love and is healed. Bernini's eloquent marble of Teresa of Avila in Rome's Santa Maria Vittoria shows a woman in rapture, her body pierced with the golden arrow or love even to her vitals. God, Designer and Lover, can, does, and will enter our bodies with complete majesty, ardent passion, and consummate joy as He decides.

A succession of great *pray-ers*, the saints, has reacted to God's lovemaking in commentaries, attempts to express feebly the depth of their mystical union with God. Unerringly, they chose the Canticle of Canticles, or Song of Songs, a scriptural praise of erotic love and ecstatic delight in embodiedness. Whatever their time, language, or locale, mystics flew to the liquid lines of the Canticle to express limpingly but lovingly the only human experience they could imagine that resembled their intense union with the divine Lover.

For the feminist mystic whose prayer experiences were so often ridiculed by male directors or theologians, the choice of the Canticle is significant and revelatory. She discovered in God's lovemaking that human love was a copy; God's mystic unitive love was the original. This God Lover was supreme Teacher as well, for to be loved by God was to be enraptured indeed, but also to experience deepest learning.

Human intercourse is a glorious attempt to mirror the instant union God produces in our bodies and hearts. Made in God's image, we yearn in intercourse to surrender to another person the gift of self, body, mind, and spirit. Sexual intercourse is our loving imitation of how God makes love. Yet it can't duplicate the totality of God's power to enter into our bodies and ignite our hearts with love. God yearns for us and desires union with us— with all of us, for we are God's condominiums.

Theology, like other sciences, is beginning to take a humbler stance, to be somewhat less dogmatic concerning what it knows about God. Like their fellow scientists, theologians admit candidly that reality may well be a lost object. Theology now looks with great attention to its major assumption that what it theologizes about will always remain mystery, God.

Though we may react with fear or shock to changing our images of God, we, too, must change as new facts and values impinge on our consciousness today. The present changes in theology may even let God back into God's world as God chooses to be, and not as we decide She must be.

To change theories and images will not mean losing our faith, for faith both precedes and presupposes theology for its interpretation. Theology never creates faith, nor does reason lead us to it. No doctrine creates faith, for faith is belief in and response to God's touch.

Sexual spirituality, as it witnesses to the touch of faith and gives it life, can make our personal theology grow and enable us to live our love in a meaningful fashion. Yet each of us lives out our theology and spirituality within a culture characterized by our own language and uniqueness. So God's touch is experienced artistically as God, the tremendous Lover, touches us according to our individual needs.

It does, then, make a difference which theology and which image of God undergird and color our spirituality. Today philosophy and theology of the human person no longer need operate from the notion of some essential nature having an existence, a model fashioned out of Plato and Augustine with Aristotelian nuances. We might instead experience ourselves today as ever *in process*, constantly transmuting phases of experience, passing into other phases, and evolving. Life, in Alfred North Whitehead's phrase, comes in drops of experience. In such a setting, God is dynamic, changing, moving with us and through us in history. This renewed image of God as our cosuffering Lover can produce an integrated body-spirit spirituality, especially if we are also open to it in prayer. It can heal our self-image and lead to a holiness that includes a sexually-integrated personality.

But what is it I love when I love thee, my God? Not the beauty of any bodily thing, nor the seasons, nor the brightness of light nor fragrance of flowers . . . not the limbs that love embraces. . . .

Yet, in a sense I *do* love light and melody and fragrance and food and embrace when I love you, my God. . . . When that light shines upon my soul which no place can contain, that voice sounds which no time can take from

me, I breathe that fragrance that no wind scatters, I eat the
food not lessened by eating, and I lie in the embrace that
satiety never comes to sunder. This it is that I love when I
love my God.

—Augustine of Hippo

6

Sexual Lifestyles

As he picked up the teacup, Tony's hand shook a bit, and his voice was too loud in a nonstop stream of talk. I had been his friend and counselor for three years, so I plunged in. "Tony, what's on your mind?" The cup bounced as he set it down hard with a relieved sigh and blurted, "I thought you'd never ask!"

I laughed in reply and he went on. "You know, ordination is three weeks away, and I need to talk to somebody about this, because I can't keep going over it in my head." He hesitated; then: "I'm gay and I haven't been able to share that with anybody on the ordination committee, and now I don't know if that's dishonest or not. If I do come out of the closet, they won't ordain me, I'm sure." Tony's words poured out in a painful torrent, and the tears weren't far behind.

Why would this thirty-year-old have to hide his sexual orientation from even his closest friends and mentors? Because of society's fear of a sexuality that might be "different." Ministers and priests are supposed to be "holy" people; a sexual preference other than heterosexual is inappropriate for them, though intercourse in heterosexual marriage is permitted for ministers. But many Christian theologians hold that it belongs only there in marriage, with no extramarital activity if we are to be "moral." And as for the gay-lesbian orientation itself? Not "normal," especially for people thinking of ministry. How could they possibly help others with *their* sexual problems?

Tony was ordained after a painful encounter with the ordination committee, and he later found the counseling he wanted. But when he met his parish they couldn't accept a gay minister, so he had to leave the congregation. Today he's on the national staff of his denomination.

Behind his story lie all the old questions: What is sexuality? What constitutes "normal" sexuality? What does sexuality mean for becoming a complete human being? What does God think about sex? And, especially, what's the purpose of it all: sex, spirit, thought, labor? What's it all about, Alfie?

What fascinates me about Tony's story and its outcome are the strong feelings and the violent actions provoked by his gay orientation, as if we had all neatly packaged, adequate answers to those stiff questions above. Alive and well was a "theology of arrogance" that decided and acted with absolute surety about matters that still perplex the best scientists—and saints!

Examining the assumptions of that theology, we find a distortion of the importance of heterosexual genital married activity that turns it into a mechanical performance of the only permitted kind. We thereby sin against truth and tolerance because we don't have all the data in on what constitutes "normal" sexual conduct; we don't know enough to make a definitive moral judgment about *all* forms of sexual conduct. So we end up exploiting, manipulating, and misusing sexuality, strangling its coflowering with the spirit. Idolizing heterosexual intercourse as the sole criterion of normal sexual relationship is another instance of the pornographic mind because it emphasizes one expression of sexuality as the only valid vehicle for love.

In selecting and living out a sexual lifestyle, how can we avoid this arrogance and still evaluate critically the various styles available to us today? Tony's congregation, for instance, saw his orientation as immoral; Tony himself did not. What criteria were used? How can we decide among so many conflicting opinions, dogmas, and pronouncements, often made with fierce certainty?

In our time sex is often a matter of jokes, fear, and guilt, rather than an expression of joyful, caring love. We know, too, that the misdirected power of sexual feeling can explode into anger and panic rather than be released as liberating, sensuous enjoyment. So the questions and the answers are pushed by the pressure of actual crises, difficult decisions, and the need for certainty.

Consequently, many of us have learned not to rejoice in the ecstasy of oneness that sexuality can bring, not to understand it as training in becoming a feeling, loving friend, as Jesus is. Sexuality is an education in how to be human, how to be open and vulnerable, not hiding behind facades and pride; it opens us to growth and learning how to love. Yet some writers have through their pronouncements made it into a most dangerous activity. Books of moral theology (ethics) are still often about what *not* to do in order not to sin.

Moral decisions are often made in the name of religion. Yet valid religious experience is, first of all, *human* experience. Historically we've learned to call religious those parts of life that are mysterious, beyond comprehension, because they are so other. They send us in search of the sacred and the transcendent. Calling ourselves religious but denying these dimensions of life makes us the opposite. And in the opinion of Anthony Padavano, if one responds to these aspects of life, even if not as a member of a formal religion, one thereby becomes religious.

All valid religious experience sends us on a search for two precious jewels: freedom and fidelity—excellent criteria for judging the worth of our decisions. Freedom is the right and ability to do what we feel we must do to be human. Fidelity finds us using freedom to be what we choose to be even though others may not agree with how we interpret that choice.

Freedom and fidelity serve our goal of becoming radical lovers. The agony and ecstasy of good decision making means using freedom in search of a commitment to what makes our life meaningful. Chosen commitments free us and allow us to stop thrashing about, never arriving at God's heart within our own. Commitment centers our energies and releases them for action.

Radical love implies a use of faithful freedom with these criteria in mind: presence to and respect for our friends, caring for their integrity, and the giving and receiving of self in concern in order to live as Jesus did. These criteria for faithful, loving decision making would seem to apply to any lifestyle, any sexuality. Love is the central tenet of Christianity. Are we to assume that homosexuals/bisexuals don't or can't so love? Can't, then, be Christian?

Love as humanizer can make sexuality a powerful aid for living in faithful freedom, just as love must sometimes humanize spirit to integrate its kind of response to God's call. Here the possible meaning of our individual uniqueness, our See-Levels, becomes clearer. God seems to be in love with difference; He makes so much of it! Not one of us is like any other. Our God is not threatened by different ways to express his gift to us of human sexuality. Our God is so messy. He so loves variety!

But difference in sexual expression can threaten us; we don't have a God's eye-view just yet. In fact, one sign of growth in breadth of personality is that ability to include more and more different others in our acceptance range. The size of our character thereby grows, and so does our capacity to love. Jesus was a totally actualized person with a full-size personality. He could tolerate incredible differences and uniqueness; he seemed to thrive on it, for in it he saw his Father's hand, his endless creativity: endless varieties of lovers in our endless varieties of human personality so that we can uniquely care for one another.

We can relate God's tolerance for difference to the question of the morality of homosexual orientations. We're persons with particular sexual orientations, preferences, and types of activity. Gay-lesbian *orientation*, then, does not mean inordinate, subnormal sexual activity any more than does heterosexual. Each of us loves uniquely, shaping our sexual-spiritual lives with our God-given powers. To respect that variety, we need to say "homosexualities," because differences are just as prevalent among gays and lesbians as in the "straight" community. Some gays are faithful, some are not; some gays are wanting in commitment and faithful freedom, some are not. So also for the lesbian orientation.

As our homosexual brothers and sisters publicly declare their orientation, church and society must come to terms with these issues of justice, love, and respect for difference. We need an ethics and a moral theology based on the actual sexual human situation and not on assumptions and mythology from the past. In the light of our ignorance of what constitutes normal human sexuality, can we continue to make definitive moral judgments about what we don't completely understand?

For example, biology and genetics still debate over sex differentiation and no one yet knows definitely if homosexual tendencies are innate, learned, or induced by hormonal triggers.

For more data for the study of psychospiritual life we may look to brain research in the eighties. Yet the psychological researchers still give differing answers to questions basic to decisions about sexuality. Is the brain different in men and women? If so, at what stage of development does it become so? Is sexual orientation a matter of nature or nurture? Are people gay or lesbian because of how nature shaped them or because of conditioning?

The hypothalamus *is* differently sexed, according to Prof. Diane McGuinness of the University of California, Santa Cruz. She feels it's almost certainly differently stamped before birth by sex hormones that develop at puberty. We also know from Stanford University researchers that some sex differences seem to be independent of culture—for example, the ways information is gathered and problems are solved. In the brain, they feel, from the beginning are woman's sensitivity to sound and people and man's interest in objects, spatial dimension, light, and patterns.

Yet research indicates that these statistical differences between males and females are extremely minor compared with differences among people of the *same* sex. In fact, eighty to ninety-five percent of all variations observed among people occur among men as a group, and among women as a group.

If we apply this information to the question of gay-lesbian orientation, cut-and-dried statements or decisions do not seem to fit that orientation—any more than they fit heterosexuals' activity sexually. Some counselors say that their gay-lesbian clients are merely confused; others, that they have "castration anxiety" or fear of female genitals. Yet many homosexual people also engage in heterosexual intercourse. They have perhaps, then, a bisexual orientation, one that may someday prove characteristic of many people—depending on how we as a society and as church develop our attitudes about the purpose and meaning of sexuality.

Trying to gather some fairly reliable data, then, is the first step in making a moral judgment about anything, not just sex. And clear data seem hard to come by, since some scientists claim homosexuality is a disease; others, a brain-induced condition; and still others, arrested development, hormonal imbalance, or just plain conditioning.

However, the 1981 Kinsey Report from Indiana University shows that homosexuality may be determined at birth by biology and that about ten percent of all children are born with a strong "gender nonconformity," a failure to like what others of their sex like. It's not learned, contrary to the findings of the 1979 Masters and Johnson study.

The Kinsey group found that homosexuality cannot be traced to a psychological or social pressure but is a "very deeply rooted set of impulses and yearnings . . . needs and feelings," with the signs showing as early as four years old.

Important for the moral question is the 1965 Kinsey Report on sex offenders, however. It found that the use of force is rare among gays and lesbians; it seems to be a prerogative mainly of heterosexuals. The report found that gays and lesbians are, in general, less violent than heterosexuals.

These findings work against our tendency to lump all of humanity into polar opposites: homosexual and heterosexual. Yet an early Kinsey Report in 1948 on sexuality among American males showed a wide continuum from exclusively heterosexual to exclusively homosexual behavior. Sexual preference can be rated on the same scale as behavior. But the two are not always in line. All of us need to restore wholeness and consistency between what we really prefer and how we behave sexually. The old performance-syndrome really operates here. That's why a number one question in counseling always is: "What do you really want?" Seeing all sexual lifestyles along a wide continuum of preference and behavior, and not cut into two varieties only, can eliminate ideas that gays and lesbians are wholly different from everyone else, a "they" as opposed to "us." Christianity in its finest hour knows no stranger, no "they." Our present period could be one of those hours for the churches and society as well, a chance for growth and understanding through permitting what we now call "difference," allowing for a pluralism in sexual lifestyles in a nation committed to pluralism, and thus not judging before the time.

Yet church people along with the general population are afraid of the gay-lesbian lifestyle and ask, How can gays and lesbians live their love of God and neighbor in a holistic spirituality? In a church? Yes, of course, they can and they do. Many of them are, of course, open, generous, compassionate, kindly people serving church and society every day. They have been for years, and centuries!

A few criteria for determining sexual right and wrong in a given situation may help. Long ago Thomas Aquinas summarized centuries of moral thinking in a threefold standard for judging behavior: (1) done for the right purpose; (2) done with the right person (spouse!); (3) done in the right way (heterosexual intercourse). On December 1, 1983, the new Vatican statement on sex appeared, repeating over and over that *love* is to be the characteristic of authentic sex, with personal maturity the goal of "rightful sexual communion." "Sexuality, oriented, elevated and integrated by love . . . is achieved in the full sense only with the realization of affective maturity."

The document shows some real changes since Aquinas's position above. For him, sex "for the right purpose" meant just one thing: procreation. But the 1983 document feels that sexual intercourse has a twofold value: an intimate communion of love between the couple, and the fostering of children, with unity ahead of fecundity this time! It recognizes, too, the great challenge involved in integrating one's sexuality and spirituality, the demanding work of fusing genitality, eroticism, and love.

Homosexuality, however, is still described in the document as impeding the person's acquisition of sexual maturity, and not a likely path to sexual integration. So the documents come and go in a long line of statements about how to live our sexual moral lives. We respect their wisdom, but we are left with our conscience in our hands, as Thomas More put it, and *we* are responsible for deciding.

So, back to decision making! We should remember one point exemplified above: There are no "pure" facts; the facts are always somewhat inadequate. Waiting until one is absolutely certain is fruitless and frustrating; it can also be avoidance, for not to decide is also a decision. Every moral judgment and decision is an experiment. So we gather what *data* we can humanly obtain, then we ask about the *motive*: Why should I do or not do this? Then comes my *intention*: What do I desire to attain in this act? And, finally, the *results*: What will be the consequences and how am I responsible for them? So we can bring sexual intercourse into some focus by evaluating it according to these three questions and the always relevant question: How does this act fulfill my commitment to live Jesus' value system? How just is it? How loving?

Another listing of questions can throw light on the dark areas of our decision in a given situation:

- What is the *normal* behavior about this question in this society? Is it changing now? What data do we have? What biases and prejudices exist? (Input from culture, science)
- What do the *laws* say about it? Are they changing? (Input from codes)
- What does our own *conscience* have to say about it? Consulting with others?
- What does *God* seem to think about it when we ask in prayer? When we are still and listen? In Scripture?

Applying these questions for ethical decisions to sexual orientation or activity can be helpful, for they push us to be honest—the bottom line, the real pain level in trying to decide. We try to see the truth as best we can, after thought, consultation, prayer, looking into God's eyes to see if we can borrow some of his enormous tolerance for difference—even our own! We use in adult fashion that conscience of ours, the meeting place for ethics and morality. It brings intuition and reason together with contemplative listening to God, and that is the best try we humans can make. But that best try presupposes the daily habit of asking God for the gift of discernment or right decision, a gift of understanding God wants to give us.

Getting our conscience in shape through consulting God daily about everything, not just sexual decisions, enables us to operate in the new, truly pluralistic world that's being born. Tolerant of difference, prayer deepens a radical love that embraces the lover's uniqueness and holds us to a commitment to faithful loving. It teaches us how to select and live our sexual orientation with justice and love. It leads us to examine any theological basis that works against acceptance and tolerance for the orientations of others—especially because radical love accepts my neighbors as the actual persons they are. It takes a firm position of accepting their otherness, their right to be themselves, with a different See-Level from mine, a different way to see and interpret the world. It is radical because it cuts to the root (radix) of my unconscious demand that the neighbor be like me! Radical, too, because it allows them to be radically who they actually are, God's idea. To that we say Yes, no matter how hard that idea might be to understand—or embrace! No wonder Jesus was the truest of all revolutionaries: He taught radical love!

Practicing such a love begins with accepting where others really are. It means that some Christian theological teaching about homosexuality may need reexamination. The 1976 Catholic Bishops' letter "To Live in Christ Jesus" says, "Homosexual activity, however, as distinguished from homosexual orientation, is morally wrong." Activity is declared morally wrong because it's assumed that some kinds of homosexuality are curable. This attitude seems to ignore some of the data we've looked at above.

The letter says further that homosexual activity is not natural for anyone and is therefore not morally justified. Basic assumption: Because "they lack an indispensable finality (biological procreation potential) these acts are instrinsically disordered and can in no way be approved." Yet in Catholic teaching since Vatican II, including the new 1983 letter, more than procreation may be intended in sexual activity: "an intimate communion of love between the couple." So why not a loving gay or lesbian couple?

Luther said well that the church is always having to be
reformed. Especially its theory of self and God. When they
wrote their letter, the Catholic bishops started with an unproven
assumption: that the only morally acceptable way of living one's
sexual love was heterosexual and in marriage—because it's open
to creating new life. They assumed they knew what "natural"
sexuality was.

In an overpopulated world how strange is this emphasis on
procreation! The Hebrew proscription of homosexuality
implied that it was immoral because it did not provide new lives
for the tribe. Implied in the bishops' letter, too, is a view of
marriage as the only acceptable expression of genital sexuality,
yet marriage is a social form rapidly changing today. More
important, the letter seems to assume that *within* marriage
moral violations of love are unknown: rape, physical abuse,
spiritual and psychic violence. Are these moral aberrations to
be preferred to sexual relations expressing love and commitment between loving persons of the same sex?

A more pluralistic spirituality needs an intelligent and humble theology that is aware of all available data, critical of its own
historical assumptions, designed to promote love in the church
community, and concerned about whether or not people are
caring for one another. That theology will mean educating all of
us through pulpit, radio, and TV to speak out against the
injustices rampant in sexism—including attacks against the
homosexual person. Theology is finally beginning to be aware
of the plight of women in the churches—another rampant form
of sexism. But this skirmish is a fine preparation for taking on a
bigger one: *all* sexual intolerance.

We need to say clearly that homosexuality is not sexual
depravity freely chosen. Nor is it an infection passed on to
young people. We must deny that all homosexuals are violent
and given to crime. We need to welcome the homosexual sister
or brother into Christian communities with the same social
rights and privileges as any other member. Why are they forced
to found their own "Christian" churches? Since when is one's

sexual orientation the prime criterion for church membership?

Part of the agenda of all Christian churches struggling with shaping a theology of sexual love will have to be a close look at the present form of marriage—surely not the totally "Christian" lifestyle it's presumed to be. The report "Human Sexuality" of the Catholic Theological Society of America considers other morally acceptable expressions of the sexual-spiritual life besides today's heterosexual marriage form.

Again, such a critique needs valid criteria, whether we are examining a social form like marriage or a disease like sexism. The deepest criteria remain justice and love in the relationship, no matter which genders are involved. Truly moral relationships express mutual, non-coercive love, care, and respectful concern for growth in the integrity and personhood of the beloved. These form the basis for friendship and foster mutuality to help both partners grow more human, and, so, more holy. The Society's report emphasizes the quality of the relationship as crucial: "Christian morality does not require a dual standard. Gays and lesbians enjoy the same rights and incur the same obligations as the heterosexual majority. They are required to examine and evaluate their behavior in the light of the same values and characteristics of wholesome human sexuality."

Some of these values and characteristics we've seen above, but we don't assume that we've got them all in a box. More work needs to be done: What is the purpose, the goal, the meaning of our being embodied, ensexed? Let's keep that open. Science can help us with data to reshape theology's basic assumptions; we've seen this in the change in Catholic thought from Aquinas to Vatican II. Just as political revolutionaries working toward human liberation in Nicaragua and El Salvador contribute their life experience of trying to live the gospel, so people there must translate the Scriptures for their kind of love story with God, their struggle to be faithful and free, to be human. Such people who try to be honest about what they experience, to call out that the emperor has no clothes, have always been the prophets for the rest of us too busy to notice. So Christian

churches are now going through the process of using all these
data to reshape their theories of sexual spirituality, marriage,
woman's role, and human liberation.

In the past, churches have had to rethink and change their
stand on slavery and on divorce. Now churches must rethink
the question of war in a nuclear age. Again, we must ask the
basics: What does human experience tell us about any sexual
practice? What do married people—or singles (the neglected
masses!)—tell us about the meaning of their sexual experience?
These important data can shape a theology of *eros* to fit real
human sexual experience with neighbor and God, not some
preconceived textbook concept of what sexuality means. How
can each of us take responsibility (move through our conversion
experience) for mutual justice and love in our sexual lifestyle,
no matter what its form? That is always the bottom line.

Out of the suffering of gay-lesbian communities today may
come great insights for all of us. That lifestyle and orientation
asks questions that have needed asking for centuries. What is
normal sexuality? If we don't fully know, why do we beat, kill, or
vilify people whose orientation is not ours? Fear? Panic?
Scapegoating? In living a Christian life, isn't faithful caring for
another's good a more valid criterion than heterosexual intercourse? Jesus doesn't condemn sexual lifestyle; he is busy with
more important things. He seems more interested in justice,
care for others, responsible use of freedom, tolerance for difference, openness to risk and sharing, and the ability to recognize our own trapped narrowness, prejudice, and bigotry.

Sin to him is alienation from one another and God, refusing
to allow anyone different views, customs, lifestyles, refusing to
experience life or to grow, change, fail, and meet God in the
world. Sexual love for him is part of the gift of life to be used,
like every gift, with responsibility for practicing justice and love
toward oneself and the beloved.

Today's sexual revolution implies a discontent, in spite of
some of its negative features, with the assumptions of sexual
right and wrong inherited from 2,000 years of ethical moral
decisions usually handed down by celibate males. In a world

freezing to death for lack of love, how ridiculous to insist that there is only *one* legitimate way to express sexual love! Jesus' command to love one another doesn't describe one particular sexual expression. The witness of many faithful, loving relationships of gays and lesbians today, then, may be God's way of making us examine some assumptions about sexuality, love, marriage, and spirituality. If we assume we're here on earth to learn how to accept and give love, their experience can be valuable additional data about what love can mean.

Today many Christian gay and lesbian couples bring to their church communities their desire to make a commitment to one another and to ratify it before a community in a "holy union." Can we assume that God is displeased with that? I suspect that God is not upset about homosexuality; but we are. Nor does God, though responsible for sexuality itself, seem a bit guilty about it. The embodied, ensexed human models keep right on coming into this world.

Gay and lesbian holy unions are a type of marriage expressing the same goals as heterosexual ones—faithful love and commitment in a just, loving relationship. Trouble with this notion may come because we assume that Christian heterosexual marriage has always been as we know it. Yet it was not until the Council of Trent (1565) that the church declared a Christian ceremony necessary for a valid marriage!

We can question the present social form of heterosexual marriage, its roots and evolution: Can its troubles indicate its imminent change into multiple forms of expression, and not *one* solely acceptable form? The roots of marriage lie in the early church reacting to cultural pressures to combine Jewish, Greek, and Indian ideas of marriage. The church preserved the legal familial marriage and made it monogamous. So the church outlawed divorce, and, illogically enough, forbade concubinage, combining Jewish insistence on procreation and Greco-Indian ideas of sexual abstinence in a "Christian" form of marriage. We confused the state of chastity (an ideal of the time) with the profane arranged institution of civil marriage. No glue could hold that mixture together forever. As soon as

Christian zeal cooled and church became part of state, concubinage and prostitution returned. Marriage as a Christian
idea was further transformed in the Middle Ages by the cult of
courtly love, which gave birth to some aspects of the romantic
concept of marriage we have today.

For Paul, marriage made holy the sexual feelings between
spouses. But the church taught that the sacred element in
marriage was fidelity of the partners to a contract. And this law
of fidelity was supposed to develop one's humanity. Paul got
angry at those who would make the law a god, who thought that
people could only be trusted to be faithful if there were a law or
contract.

But marriage is an historical social form, not an absolute.
New roles for women will certainly change it; but no matter
how marriage changes, it still needs a friendship-based theology—which it has never had. Modeled on Roman forms,
marriage today is an amalgam of different cultural views of both
love and sexuality, conditioned by politics and economics
always—for example, by the emergence of the middle class and
by the Industrial Revolution.

Protestant theologies of marriage have been helpful as anti-
dote to the Catholic variety; they were at least written by
married males. Yet Protestant scholars, too, swing from theories
of dualism to sexism, to overemphasis on genitality, to personal
loving union. No wonder, given the amalgam of historical
elements they had to try to incorporate. Today's process theology seems more helpful in its view of persons as dynamic
becomings, with God's image in us as our capacity to love.
Norman Pittinger's approach stresses love as central to sexual
expression, with fidelity intrinsic to the union.

Can we develop—or do we wish to develop—a theology from
useful elements of Jewish, Catholic, Protestant, and Eastern
views that can transcend those fixed elements: a male-female
sexual-spiritual committed relationship? If *person* transcends
sexuality always, and if it is the *union of persons* that needs both
a new theory and a new social form, then the best of historical
theologies of marriage may provide some resources. Although

we need always to be aware of today's changing social and sexual conditions, this theology must be based on faithful commitment to live in justice and love in union with God and one another, no matter what the sex of the partner. The way would be open, then, to create forms to incorporate the loving expressions of gays and lesbians into Christian theologies of loving union.

Some questions for analyzing assumptions about today's marriage structures must first be asked:

• What does the marriage form assume about human being? Is it possibly based on a perfectionist model that insists that one could not possibly be mistaken in this call to marriage?

• Does the present marriage form allow for continuing *conversion experiences* for the couple as God calls? Are persons placing their primary commitment to God's call, which could allow for change, being called to another lifestyle?

• Can we look upon annulment and divorce as sometimes necessary closure forms, and not failure certificates? If so, why are they not done in the spirit of reconciliation, so that these ending experiences will have fitting prayer and liturgy to help people move through such major change?

• Could liturgical, prayerful ending ceremonies help effect the healing so needed after a separation? Why is the religious experience of prayer and healing not used as a person pursues a different call from God?

• Could the churches, aided by separated persons' experiences, regularly provide such public or private ceremonies of healing as valid rites of passage to fit a changing gift-call? Would the healing dimension of prayer and acceptance by a community help a person move through the experience?

Both the woman's movement and homosexual unions call for the reexamination of today's concept of marriage. Subject to change, it needs to move toward structures that can provide the intimacy, the sheltering of love, and the support of commitment that will respect difference, that will recognize women as equally human persons with men, and foster mutual growth in justice and love. Marriage today is an ambiguous label, however. Some marriages are financial, social convenience structures; some merely provide legalized prostitution; others try for full equality of partners and endure the punishment society inflicts for cracking stereotypes of what a macho husband and a motherly wife should be.

It is a fact that man has attained his humanity and has humanized his sexuality only through the discipline . . . of the conjugal institution.

. . . Marriage is, in our civilization, always to some degree under the mark of duty.

Many people are defeated by it. Marriage can protect the duration and the intimacy of the sexual bond, and therefore render it human. But it can also be what ruins for many both its duration and its intimacy.

—Paul Ricoeur

In our time when every social form rocks with value change, married people struggle to build a spiritual-sexual life while handling personal value shock. But that shock signals responsibility for reexamining our lifestyles to see if they're serving love. If they are not, changes may be in order. One half of the marriage partnership, woman, may decide to claim her equal humanity, her responsibility to discover and follow God's call to her to use her gifts. If she does, then the church must take that major world change into account in interpreting what shape marriage should take and what is morally acceptable in sexual unions.

An important help for women claiming that equal humanity and responsibility is the fine work of women like Carol Gilligan of Harvard University. Her study in contrasting ways of defining and developing morality, *In a Different Voice,* published in 1982, is required reading for the student of developing sexual morality. She provides the other side of Lawrence Kohlberg's study based on male development and urges women to appreciate their tendency to see the world in terms of *connection,* relationships, and intimacy. Claiming and valuing this tendency is part of the *human* enterprise, not just woman's. It provides psychological grounding for the gospel call to love everyone as potential friend and to see no one as enemy.

Many marriages do not serve justice and love; many new forms of sexual relationship appear to. Woman now claims her right to friendship with her partner. A plurality of differing forms would seem in order to fit these changing developments.

The classic favorite of the mystics, The Song of Songs, can offer scriptural comfort for a married spirituality. Helmut Gollwitzer sees the canticle as the celebration of sexual love, and possibly married love, while he also faces the inevitable institutional nature of marriage pointed out by Ricoeur above.

> *Eros* (sexual love) enters into *agape* (divine love) when sexual love takes place between two persons who acknowledge one another as equals and who know that because their love is human, so also it is fully spiritual. . . .
>
> Here is a love that knows no separation of physical and spiritual. . . . So all our attempts to structure sexual *eros* must be considered as helps, not conditions. Love is not legitimized by legal sanctions. . . . It needs no marriage license or church ceremony . . . yet it will be institutionalized.

7

Scandalous Time

For everything there is a season and a time for every matter
under heaven: a time to be born, and a time to die; . . . a
time to break down, and a time to build up; . . . a time to
cast away stones, and a time to gather them together; . . .
a time to embrace, and a time to refrain from embracing; a
time to seek, and a time to lose; a time to keep, and a time
to cast away.

—Ecclesiastes 3:1-6

Changing lifestyles can be threatening; so we need a good
theory about what such change may mean. A helpful idea in
regard to change is the "temporary call"—the call to follow a
particular path until such time as the Spirit may through
people, events, and situations call us down a different path.

Linked to the idea of temporary call is the data available on
modern life expectancy. "Until death do us part" was possible
and sensible for ancient people who expected to be dead by
thirty-five. We live longer today and have two or three "lives."
So the question is how to live them all well. The idea of a
temporary call can help us make sense of today's changing
lifestyles.

Time really is a "scandal" to us because time means we have
only so long to live. So the words of Ecclesiastes above ask us to
surmount the scandal of time and stay open for God's signal to
change, to move on, to go with the river. Again, the very fact
that God may call us to change can be a really painful *scandalum* (stumbling block). Why must *we* change?

It's very natural that change frightens us, since flexibility is
the most difficult to acquire of all the characteristics of adult
behavior. We think we have found our niche, and suddenly a
voice says, "Come!" That can be scandalous, a source of fear

and reproach. Why does God do this to us? Because if we are not called out of our velvet ruts, we may well stagnate there. God who knows the heart knows the time to change it as well.

One Buddhist view of life divides it into different periods (as in *Siddhartha*), to which different sexual-spiritual lifestyles are appropriate. That view may be useful for us now. Why not see life as a process in which our sexual lifestyle adjusts as we change in age, desires, work, and health?

We're told that life gives us three challenges: sexuality, possessions, and pretensions. Could each one call for a different lifestyle for its agenda: marriage or committed union; then perhaps a celibate period; and possibly a contemplative time, grounding involvement with social justice and service?

If theologies of marriage need reexamining for—among many factors—their over-emphasis on heterosexual intercourse as chief value, they also need to give a wider place to other healing dimensions of marriage, like communion, sensuous acceptance of life, and androgynous attitudes. The temporary vocation theory may help question marriage as necessarily "forever" if we apply to it a theory of God's gifted call. Any vocation lasts as long as God gives gifts to carry it out.

Sue and Anne, my friends, had taken each other in a committed, exclusive holy union. Having consulted, prayed, searched, they had discovered their lesbian orientation *after* divorcing their husbands. Their household then consisted of the two women parents and a total of four children. Theirs was a new definition of marriage, yet lived within the image of what society expected marriage to be: two people committed exclusively to each other, raising their children in a common household.

Models like this one abound. People are trying to work through sexual orientation and the lifestyle that it will call for. When the holy union failed, as it did after some six years, neither Sue nor Anne could blame the break on the type of lesbian relationship they shared. Rather, they broke up because of a *personality* conflict, a communications problem—just like many other marriages! One partner wanted to consume an incredible amount of the other's time and attention. Anne, as a professional, couldn't fulfill Sue's expectations because of her career schedule. Further, they disagreed about the best way to raise children: One was a disciplinarian; the other, permissive and easy.

They had fully resolved to be together "for life" as one family, but their temperamental and philosophical differences finally broke them apart. Obviously they did not have for each other the gift of marriage, the giving and receiving of persons that brings both to gradual spiritual growth and to deeper union with God and each other. Rather, as in heterosexual marriage, the reasons for their separation were grounded in ineradicable differences of personality, attitudes, and, especially, values. Their satisfactory sex life could do nothing to salvage that difference. Their problems were human differences that did not stem from the fact that these two committed people were lesbians. These two people had perhaps a temporary call to be together and do the learning that time together was to bring them. They hoped to part as friends.

A theology of gifts makes a priority of whatever God is asking us to do and be; for God, as dynamic energy, can move us into new places and roles. In the past, the focus has been on gritting one's teeth to stick to a lifestyle forever. Instead, we can stay open to listen to life to see how God is working in our lives. And sometimes that means changing lifestyles, even marriage, in order to follow the Spirit's call carefully discerned in justice and love. Change is scary; yet, after all, to be human is to be temporary, to be on the road to the biggest change of all.

Temporariness simply names an important aspect of our humanity: immersion in time, that strong shaping factor in our conversion process as well. Time, says the Chinese proverb, is a race with pain. But it is more. It can also be a joyful journey with God in loving listening to his Spirit's guiding voice.

Alertness to God's signals mapping that journey in the events of life is the secret of valid change of lifestyle. As we daily give ourselves to God in surrendering prayer, listening as we quiet our images and thoughts and rest in her arms, we come back to the grind again, empowered for the journey. And God teaches us whether to go or to stay—if we will but listen with the inner ear of love.

> Nothing is more seductive for us than freedom-of-conscience, but nothing is a greater cause of suffering. . . . In place of the rigid, ancient law, we must hereafter with free heart decide for ourselves what is good and what is evil, having only Thy image before us as our guide.
> —F. Dostoevski

People today must say yes or no to freedom and responsibility. We are asked to accept and use that most potent gift, the power to make moral decisions. In accepting the gift lies our potential for wholeness, the fruit of faithful freedom and growth in love. And always God's image does and will guide us.

Choices are particularly painful, as we have seen, in regard to ending a marriage—or rather, in regard to following God's call to a different sexual-spiritual lifestyle, to another vocation.

For instance, when we attend a wedding, we may assume that the couple taking one another in faith before God have discerned deeply. They have had their decision tested by the community for whose service this bonding takes place. We may trust that they feel called to follow the Spirit to conversion of body, heart, and mind and that each partner is and wants to be a part of the other's conversion call from God. They want to make their mutual life a gift of service and, so, an act of worship as well. Many theologies of marriage come together in the above picture, but it's hard to know which ideas are really embraced by the people involved.

But if we humans can discern and decide, we can also be in error. That's why decisions drive us crazy. They imply the risk of being wrong, when all the while we forget that risking responsibility means moving toward maturity and adulthood. For if we risk laying ourselves open to experience, we learn something about ourselves in the process. And God seems intensely interested in our learning, especially our learning to love.

What if a couple discovers over years and tears that their

marriage is not part of God's call to grow through experiencing their love? When they can face their situation honestly, not calling it failure but learning, they may also see if they really tried to put on the attitudes or mind of Christ. If so, they may decide to open their hearts to the changes to which God calls them through one another: the patience, self-giving, kindliness, and self-knowledge of which marriage is the graduate school.

After prayer, consultation, and the acid test of time, they may still discover they are called to change their promise and give way to God's new call in their individual lives—because only God's Spirit can give couples the gift of mutual love. Donald Gelpi, S.J., feels that only a marriage rooted in a gift of God for one another is fully sacramental. God's direction of their lives and obedience to his call is the couple's primary vocation. Growth in loving kindness to and concern for one another is the top criterion of their sincerity in following that call.

Will they continue to respect the former partner, trying to learn how to become friends? Time will be needed to heal the pain, but lashing oneself in one's psychic cellar over the separation helps not at all. Daily prayerful consultation with God, work with a therapist, healing exercise, meaningful work, and service are good therapy. Each partner as human being is still called to a sexual, holistic spirituality and to their primary relationship with God. There is life after divorce! No change of lifestyle changes God's deepest call to be incredibly loved by Him even when our human loves flicker and fade.

We may assume, looking back in guilt, that our promises made in marriage were dishonest or invalid. Rearview mirrors can distort pictures, especially when it comes to our past motives. Today's painful changes don't necessarily imply lack of previous commitment. They only illuminate possible inadequacies and hint at future models of improvement. Each decision can mean growth in understanding and compassion, just what we are here to learn!

Marriage may well remain a threatened lifestyle so long as

husbands do not consider their wives candidates for true friendship on a par with their male confidants. The friendship model discussed earlier applies to married as well as to single friendships, of course. It means work, time, patience; both partners are called to amounts of growing and learning that no computer could handle. But the result of honesty and hard work is the greatest human good, a true friendship!

Perhaps the chief monster in the closet of married spirituality as friendship is simply that we cannot stomach much difference. When someone else doesn't see the world as we do, it shakes our confidence. That testing and learning is painful, but then radical love is no kindergarten. Some people say love takes at least thirty years to learn. It's an adult activity, like faith or true religion!

Like any calling, then, marriage and ministry are subject first to God's enspirited urging. They can't be idolized any more than celibacy can. In times of rapid social change, lifestyles are never exempt from sweeping new directions. No lifestyle, no calling, is necessarily for life, especially one (like celibacy) imposed by church disciplinary regulation and not freely chosen in response to God's urging in the heart.

First comes answering God's call with honest discernment even if that is sometimes painful. Then lifestyle will follow from the call, and not the opposite. Neither ministry nor marriage is necessarily forever unless God so decides; they may be idols we need to topple if the community's life in the Spirit needs such a change.

Temporariness can produce wariness in most of us. Yet each year we see about one million American marriages go to the divorce court; so change is also a familiar social concept. But Christians still have trouble with changes that challenge the theologies we've been taught in home, school, and church. In this transition time we are marginal people raised in one culture and coping in another. Our values are bombarded from every side. Clear blacks and whites are gone; even the grays are fuzzy. The walls of convention no longer shore us up; we must choose, yet often we lack criteria.

Transition periods play havoc with promises that demand commitment to spouse, community, or lover. When Jim and Maria chose one another, they thereby eliminated all others and became vulnerable to being shaped by that third entity, their relationship. What really matters is the very *quality* of the relationship beneath the promise and commitment. The lack of such quality can help us decide the worth of a call.

Psychology may attribute our modern reluctance to make permanent commitments to the prolonged dependency of youth or our unwillingness to assume obligations in a bomb-threatened world. But deeper still is our lack of an adequate *theory of the human person* to support present expectations concerning Christian marriage, celibate priesthood, single life, or sexual preference.

A theology based upon the ensexed embodied human person as God's child gifted with a unique temperament and See-Level is the cornerstone for one valid approach to dealing with call. Gifts are showings forth of God's power through us for the community. So the variety of gifts carries God's powerful energy in individual servings, our unique temperaments, to the people of God.

We cannot use the gifts/calls well without the primer, learning to love, which means willingness to change as love teaches us how. This openness to change when it means listening to God's call means we're really trying to put on the mind of Jesus, to be converted. But we still need all the criteria above to help us discern how and when to change.

It is up to God where and how She wants us to use our gifts in a lifestyle. Beyond gifts as mere talents is the primary call to be the self, the person God thought about in creating us, the gift of self that we are to the world. That means using body, mind, and spirit to love the world for and with God with a radical love that permeates a valid sexual spirituality.

We may resist the idea that we are gifts for the world. Close your eyes, hug yourself, and say quietly, "Thank you, God, for the gift that I am to the world." Did you believe it? God does, and wants us to. In God's opinion we are gifts and by accepting

God's idea of us, God's love, we can radiate love in turn. We no longer fear the changes God can call us to because that conversion experience lives out our love.

Changing lifestyles brings into focus the challenge to males in this society. Men often receive little compassion for their present plight. True, they have the top jobs, the highest wages, and most of the capital and power; but their time is running out. So we must say a word for men, the walking wounded from all the world's wars—military, economic, and psychosocial.

In some ways men today may be in worse shape than women, because they must still operate in a closed system that prizes competition, success, and violent use of power as *normal* conduct for them. In this traumatic historical change time, men are ill equipped and highly threatened in particular by value changes in women. Men still live somewhat in the old system, even if part-time. Schizophrenia, added to heart attack, is a high price for straddling two worlds.

The male Christian, then, may experience threats to his sexual vulnerability if he tries to become, like Jesus, a friend to each woman he meets. God may call him to live out his sexual spirituality in ways not quite like his sister's. For instance, until recently society did not publicly label the male as sex object, but rather as user of sex objects, women. The women's revolution has freed some women to live their sexual lives as they choose. So some males declare that they themselves are the new sex objects for women's sexual needs.

This is just a logical result of women's lack of sound sexual role models in the male power class they must imitate to gain some little power. Logical, too, because men and women have never before been expected to relate to one another *as friends*. So women do not feel responsible for initiating the act of friendship with men. This results in loveless liaisons at the cost of the integrity of both men and women. The same old model with a new aggressor?

Men now experience what women have always suffered, but that does not help achieve our mutual goal to live as Jesus did, as friends in a healthy sexual-spiritual relationship. Today's permissiveness provides paradox, surely. Women, once urged to compete covertly for men, are now openly in pursuit. Some men say they don't know how to respond. So often neither sex emerges whole or happy from the new rat race.

Women, entrapped by mixed messages from the culture, can choose to be feminist (with every kind of meaning for the term) or antifeminist. Perhaps neither position can help to develop a holistic lifestyle, especially when the idea of femininity is now used to keep women in submission—in contrast to liberation (a presumed feminist characteristic).

So many women hang between Scylla and Charybdis—choosing neither, yet apologizing about their indecision. How can they make moral sexual decisions on the basis of a fuzzy concept of what it means for them to be human beings? Caught between two opposing moral systems, how can they build their own spirituality, and in the doing help their brothers and sisters? For with our brothers and sisters we rise or fall; we are not separate, but one in God's image, one humankind!

Holding fast to the concept of our *oneness* as women and men, as God's children, we can move through the present sexual revolution not as *natures* but *histories*, deriving our identity not from our sex but from our personhood. For man as well as woman, the task is to change the heart of stone for the heart of flesh. That change contains the seeds of true liberation from the dilemma of liberation. We are conditioned but not determined, for God's Spirit within can set us free. Returning to God, the Center, can light up the road to our true identity: sons and daughters of God who deal justly and lovingly with one another.

We have been conditioned, too, to seek growth, learning, progress, and self-development. These are sometimes helpful, but we can learn our meaning most profoundly in faithfulness to God's daily teaching in prayer. God in time uses time to teach us and yet transcends it as our love relationship with Him provides the beyond in time in our cultural, sexual storms.

"Know thyself" was graven over the Temple of Delphi and is still over each human heart. We become human as we surrender to God's teaching us perennial truths about our identity and how She loves us. Our experience with God melts down terms like feminist and antifeminist in the flame of contemplative repose so that we can see beyond such labels to the reality that is human being. Resting in God within us in mystical prayer, we find stepping-stones in the stream; we need not be swept away where we do not want to go. We have our identity now: we are God's lover!

Mystical contemplation is a participative way of being with God, a holistic spirituality that includes all of our being. That familiar conversation with the Beloved within makes clearer for us how to follow a call from our deepest heart.

We are all called to return to the original vocation: to be images of God upon earth through becoming friends of Jesus, to become sexual mystics intuitively understanding truths beyond human reason in the embrace of God's unifying love. An El Greco or John of the Cross may make that mystical experience comprehensible to us in images, but each of us is called to the experience—whether we can express it or not—of being sexual mystics rejoicing in our relationships, experiencing each sensuous taste, and sharing all of it with the God who gave it in contemplative joy.

When we struggle to live a particular style, we take part in shaping a *participative* ethic beyond both feminism or male chauvinism. When we daily rest in God's love, we begin to see one another differently; for in contemplation we surrender to, and participate fully in, God's lovemaking. How, then, can we help but desire our human lover's good, as we experience God's passionate embrace? How can we ever misuse another human person who participates with us in God's love? Sharing in love asks for justice and caring, and finally for conversion, a change of behavior, so we respect and cherish our friends rather than pursue them as sexual objects. We will have, with Gregory of Nyssa, "new eyes for new suns."

Another question remains for many of us. How does one handle the question of making sexual choices about extramarital or singles' genital activity? Can mysticism and prayer answer that question in the light of the radical love we're espousing?

Yes and no. Mystical surrender, experiencing God's loving touch, listening to God's instruction within can fortify us and help us make sound decisions. Yet they never preclude the use of common sense, reason, and clear judgment. In fact, they reinforce them when the mystic experience is authentic. How does a husband decide if a sexual liaison with a woman friend, for insstance, is part of growth in sexual spirituality or mere dalliance? In the heat of daily demands, that is not a simple question.

Criteria we have used before apply here. How does this behavior make us or our partner whole, integral, dignified? Still, without trivializing (or glorifying) genital sex, it's difficult to see each act of intercourse as creating some unbreakable psychological bond. The facts do not bear out such an assumption. The struggle to be faithful to one's partner in marriage can be a symbol of God's faithfulness to us, yes. But, does a sexually nonexclusive view of faithfulness go against God's intentions for these two pledged to fidelity?

The arguments go back and forth. In regard to new forms of married fidelity, we need study, honest sharing of experience, and painful self-knowledge to redefine our criteria. Prayer as part of sexual spirituality helps us by widening the meaning of sexual feeling as we experience God's lovemaking in our bodies. It leads to the full sensuous enjoyment of feeling in our bodies and the world about us and can help lessen the genital focus as the only goal of sexual human love.

We North Americans are becoming less stereotyped in our roles as masculine and feminine. This may relieve us of the pressure to prove ourselves masculine or feminine by "performing" in or out of marriage. So downgrading sex as *the* status symbol may lessen our need to perform or use others selfishly.

Honesty cuts to the bone here as always. Will extramarital relationships help both of us toward wholeness or toward schizophrenia, fear, suspicion, and guilt? It's one thing to rebel against sexual norms. It's another to know why and to be responsible for the results.

Daniel Day Williams suggests the basis for judgments about any sexual practice: "what the practice in question does to the creation of loving, mutually supporting persons who can grow in love to God and the neighbor but who also have tendencies to exploit one another, and who must find disciplines of self-protection and self-restraint for the sake of love."

Williams asks how we can survive in a culture full of sexual symbols that idolize sex without love. How can we share in this new freedom and yet still be creative, honest, and open to the discovery of our real motives, and to authentic human love?

An authentic spirituality asks us to think through to our real motives, to be open to intellectual conversion or becoming responsible for our beliefs—and for their revision if needed. Implied in today's challenge to change sexual lifestyles is the responsibility to become mature thinkers who will examine previously unquestioned sexual assumptions we may have been operating on for years. It means studying, reading, openness to others' and our own experience. We may find out that there are things we will never find out and that's all right. But we may also be freed from sexual myths that have dominated our decisions and actions.

Perhaps the final judgment on a sexual lifestyle is what it means for us, our partner, and the community. Does it make us kinder, more patient, more open to change and growth? Are we becoming compassionate (suffering with) human beings?

The Christian tradition can help us make decisions, too, by reminding us that we can know what is right or wrong through God's Spirit living within us—who can be consulted at any time. God's Spirit leads us through love toward all that it means to be human and to the best use of freedom.

Following the Spirit in prayer also means that we seek the wisdom of groups like our church community. Discernment of spirits in our lives helps us look at the consequences of our actions carefully. So, sometimes in the expression of sexual love saying no to an act of intercourse may be a true act of love, an authentic response to the Spirit's leading. When we suffer, not for suffering's sake, but rather for the sake of the other's good, we preserve their integrity and our own.

One way we know we have made a good decision is a deep joy and peace in the sense of freedom that follows. It is not always easy to discern. In fact, sometimes we feel exceeding pain. We cannot always know whether we have been deluded until after the event. But we do have a community around us, people in the body of Christ with gifts of wisdom and prophecy that we need. It's especially important to use the timetested gifts of the married members of the community who are trying to follow the Spirit. They have experienced what many young couples are going through and have survived.

Consistently helpful in decision making is listening and valuing our own feelings. Confucius felt that human feelings were more trustworthy than so-called principles of right and wrong. He felt that the natural person was more in touch than the person led only by the head, that principles were fine so long as they were balanced with human heartedness, a sense of proportion, and the humor that goes with it.

Our Western intellectually trained minds may rebel at such a notion. But from the Confucian standpoint the idea of an absolutely unchangeable commitment to principle is perhaps bravado and a striving for heroism. And it can also be total insensitivity to inner feeling, where the Spirit works.

Confucius felt that superior persons go through life without a preconceived course of action or any taboo. They merely decide for the moment what is the right thing to do.

Ultimately, moral decisions about sexual activity will have their roots in our See-Level. What have our culture, education, experience, environment, and expectations taught us to think, to feel, or to do about embodiedness and sex? To avoid the limbo of either no freedom or all license, we can look at the past experiences of the saints, people struggling to be whole and holy.

Yet we cannot simply accept the dictates of society or the opinions of moral theologians. Laws and doctrine still leave us with the responsibility to choose and from our individual moral decisions to develop our own values. But we still need models, so the lives of real people who struggled with the same questions as ours can help us—people like Augustine of Hippo or Thomas More of Chelsea.

Even those saints had a chipped edge that helped them know they needed conversion—some fault, habit, or attitude a bit twisted and in need of healing, including problems of using sexuality well. Everybody has a chipped edge, and no one ever totally gets rid of it. But it helps others, chipped too, to identify with us.

So when we sally forth from our ivory towers to do as Jesus asked—"Love one another as I have loved you"—we can come home each evening a bit bloodied from running into those chipped edges. Yet without that experience we'd never know that we too need to change. And that need for conversion is the call of God to take responsibility for our sexual-spiritual selves. That call lures us on from freedom to freedom, even though sometimes it may look like leaving freedom far behind. William James describes change of heart, or conversion, as a process "wherein a self, hitherto divided, and consciously wrong, inferior and unhappy, becomes unified, consciously right, superior and happy in consequence of the firmer hold upon religious reality."

So change of heart, seen as responsibility, may threaten us, but the results can make us "consciously right, superior and happy in consequence of the firmer hold upon religious reality." The conversion process involves four kinds of change: intellectual, moral, religious, and emotional.

Intellectual change makes us responsible for our *beliefs*, for what we cherish—not as static, but constantly reevaluated as we change. But changing beliefs and values is the challenge to theologize, to set up a new world view.

Moral responsibility requires that we make *decisions* and then act them out as a response to our beliefs and values in the direction of living our love.

Religious conversion has to do with assuming personal responsibility for answering those messages of love and direction, those inspirations, those commands of conscience God sends us—so that we may put on the mind of Jesus.

Emotional or affective change has to do with keeping our feelings *balanced*—never the same thing as not feeling them! It means claiming responsibility for our own sexuality and for the emotions that come with it, not denying them, but deciding how to use them well.

This integral conversion, taking on these fourfold responsibilities, is called holiness, proven by the constant faithful fulfillment of daily duty. It does *not* mean that we are without sin, without mistakes.

We never get the whole fourfold program completely finished in a lifetime. Jesus did; he finished it on a cross. And even he had a tough final conversion experience in the garden of Gethsemane (Matthew 26:36-46): "Let this cup pass from me!"

Some of the saints, like Thomas More, show a beautiful fidelity in thoughts, feelings, and decisions. In Tom More, holiness (wholeness) was so outstanding that Henry VIII had to remove him not only as prime minister, but from life itself. He was just too honest to have around, a walking reproach in his lifelong effort to learn those four R's (responsibilities). He had majored in loving responsibility.

Yet, like all the saints, More went to the executioner's block still with a chipped edge. Deep down lay a not totally healed part of him; and that was all right. He had learned, like Paul of Tarsus, that in his weakness God's power was made transparent. He did not have to go to his death spotless, with every column in his ledger balanced.

God asked him only to go surrendered, open, growing, loving because he was free from self-concern, the truest mark of liberty. He had learned to ask for surrender as a gift when he felt he could not surrender. The gift came, along with the power to bear the results of his conscience decision, death.

The saints are our friends and help us not because they were perfect; they had some incredibly chipped edges. Yet they learned that God was not interested in their being spotless, but was in love with the unique person each was as God's gift to the world.

We, too, in our adventure using all facets of personality, are involved in fourfold responsibility—but not as some straitlaced perfection. Nervous striving for perfection in anxiety and fear is a far cry from accepting the love, power, and healing God wants to give us.

We can still waste God's time—and ours—by insisting that God may not love us or gift us until we are perfect—until we have got rid of every bad habit, defect, chip. *Then*, we'll be ready to deal with God—but from a position of strength.

In this connection another sexual lifestyle available to Christians comes to mind: the single life, in the unmarried state or in chosen celibacy in religious communities (a different variety from the celibacy mandated by church law for Roman Catholic priests). In a 1982 retreat of the U.S. Bishops, Archbishop Rembert Weakland of Milwaukee said frankly, "The price we [Catholics] may have to pay for a celibate clergy may be too high." God may be calling Catholics to intellectual conversion, to reexamining the assumptions, the history, and the validity of church law regarding priestly celibacy. The theology of gifts may be helpful in this study.

In our present theology of office, ordination is not necessarily a celebration of the gift of celibacy. Rather, the church says a person *must* observe celibacy if he wishes to function as a priest. One explanation given is the value of this sacrifice as sublimation for a superior goal, as a gift of human sexuality to God. But how can a sacrifice be of value if it seems to rest on disdain or fear of what we offer to God?

The law of celibacy came out of the antisexual history of the early church after long struggle, but for a thousand years it was not a requirement for priesthood in the West. Could the church today be called to reexamine its laws to match a situation in which married spirituality is no longer considered second-class holiness? Lip service is given to the glory of marriage, but in reality married persons' spirituality is considered secondary because celibacy and vowed chastity are elevated to the inside track for sainthood.

If married people must study to reform their mode of sexual spirituality, marriage, why not clerics, priests, sisters, and brothers, who have vowed celibacy or unmarriedness? We all need the same kind of healing attitudes. There are not two loves, one for God and one for humans. There is only one, and one of its dimensions is called sexual love. A theology of *gifts* means God calls individuals to celibacy as a gift. How, then, can a gift be made into law? How can we tell God to give someone the gift of celibacy—and on time for ordination?

In a healthier theology, celibacy and virginity may some day be seen as callings of some permanence, like any other gift or calling. The goal will not be avoiding sex, a negative aim, but that of every other Christian life: to follow where God's Spirit leads, to be open at each moment to the changes God may call for, and to learn how to discern what those changes are through prayer, listening, and consultation with community.

If we are consistent about virginity or celibacy as gifts of God, we can see them as appropriate at certain periods of one's life and inappropriate at others. This attitude is part of not idolizing sexuality, erotic love, or the lack of it. Rather, it keeps primary our life goal to follow the Spirit's call to conversion, to change.

Part of demythologizing either sexuality or celibacy is to ask honestly: If sexuality implies relationship, then how can it be sacrificed when no relationship exists? If we approach celibacy as a sacrifice, then by analogy the body of the celibate becomes the property of God dedicated to God alone. Alan Watts asks if God is that interested in that sacrifice, or as interested as we have been conditioned to believe.

Could it be true that in this case we are confusing God with God's symbol, the tribal Father, in our images? For possessing someone's body is not a relationship necessarily. The human being is not a thing to be possessed, but a living process; not an object, but a life and a history.

No one denies that God can and does give the gift of virginity or celibacy. But honesty asks, Does God give that gift to so many people? Is it really conceivable that tribes of us are called to celibacy—and for a total lifetime?

Can celibates be honest about whether this is God's idea or an historical, cultural development canonized by a male, celibate hierarchy? Persons practicing a vow of celibacy/virginity today feel called to sanctity, a fact stated in their order's constitutions if they are "religious" (vowed persons).

But God, who happens to be the object—and subject—of that call to holiness is not a God divorced from God's own creation. Nowhere do we find that God saying, "Choose between me and nature!" God is probably not interested in some titanic struggle of sexual willpower, but in our learning to love.

John has Jesus tell us in his farewell address that he and his Father want us humans to share his joy. He even says that he wants our happiness to be full. Somehow or other this joy has been lost in sexual, athletic asceticism and in certain kinds of monasticism. We find it, too, in the view of marriage as an inferior form of spirituality in which sexual love is only permitted for some higher good (procreation).

Honesty for the married, the religious, the celibate, and the single is based on humility, even modesty, that make pretensions to neither ascetical athletics nor contests of will. At the same time, it practices contemplative attention. We remain open to how God will summon and seduce each of us, each unique woman and man, to live out our love story with Him. In the light of this call, sexual preference is, finally, of secondary importance.

> The first principle of a Christian sexual ethic is that this side of life should be so ordered, disciplined, and released that sexual-love becomes a creative aspect of a life of *agape*: the giving of each person in service to God and his neighbor. This principle holds whether the sexual life is fulfilled in overt expression, or within a vocation of celibacy and renunciation.
>
> —Daniel Day Williams

Could, then, part of the emotional conversion of religious

orders be a rethinking of their theology of the vows, seeing them as celebrations of gifts of some permanence? This could also permit a married membership. Then members moving on to follow God's call to different sexual lifestyles would not be treated as shameful or unfaithful, but as honest seekers, still friends of Jesus and of their former companions. Why not a warm, kindly ceremony of closure for their departure, like that of their entrance and clothing? Is not God to be obeyed in her calling people to other ways of life more than our desire for large numbers of people in our communities? Don't we really prefer to accept and retain only those to whom God has given gifts for community?

Above all, where is the loving, grateful closure ceremony of public acknowledgment for the diocesan priest who moves into another lifestyle? Why is he suddenly forgotten, even financially, with no respect for what God could be doing in his life and that of the church in which he still desires to serve? If God really runs our church, why do we punish those who try to follow his call to conversion? So luminous is the halo attached to celibacy that we can fail even in love, our first task. Is our first criterion for holiness absence of genital activity? Jesus said we would know his disciples by their love for one another. What is our touchstone?

Social structures blessed by the church—like religious orders, philosophical communities, priesthood, ministry, marriage—are temporary forms set up by temporary earthlings to achieve the goal of becoming lovers like Jesus. When structures no longer fulfill those goals, they decline and die away. Such is the lesson of history. When structures no longer meet our needs, we are in a scandalous time, so we stumble and suddenly have to watch our step. We see the temporariness of our structure as new forms take over. That's normal and good because structures are habits of a group made up of changing people.

We get stuck in our structures and identify with them so much that we lose sight of the fact that *we* made them. Structures are our creatures; we are not theirs. But we soon believe the opposite. If we live in them long enough, they start to own us, instead. Person is prior to structures and the cultural forms we create to fulfill our needs and goals. We can let the structures go if God wants. Someone else can dream the dream in another generation and start over afresh.

The project for the twenty-first century needs chipped, humble lovers—lovers who not only reform our ideas of holiness in spirituality and sexuality, but also face up to what God may be doing in our embodied design, in the self that we humans are. God may be asking each of us to be responsible for the discovery and use of our *personal* gifts, those enabling calls of energy for serving others and building a new world.

To achieve that project, women and men will produce a new *human* consciousness through their sexual-spiritual lives. We hope that the concept of temporariness as *listening to God* will be one of the inclusive male-female values passed on to young people and their children. Parents will refuse to warp children's consciousness or mold them in false stereotypes—of masculine/ feminine or of separateness from nature—as the one way to live. Nor will they condition children to suppress their personal gifts in order to obey the demands of male-dominated cultural values.

Imagine the conversion parents will be called to. How difficult it is to go against cultural values that warp our environment! In the future, as parents look to the mind of Jesus and honestly face the learning available in their bodies, minds, and spirits, they will also create new models of family. No family in history has ever been faced with such an overwhelming challenge.

Consider that we are talking about changing in every way the sexual spiritual attitudes of the king and queen pins of the universe: men and women! The psychological change alone will be tremendous, as if from a new Mt. Everest on January 1 of A.D. 2000 each human being on earth suddenly saw every other with 20-20 vision, truly "new eyes for new suns" would be ours!

Temporariness, then, can be a means to that end, the humble acknowledgment of the changing human situation, for we are guests of time. Life is a bridge we use, but it is fatal to build our house on it. It cannot take the weight of immortality. Today we know that our planet is just such a bridge. Its temporariness is startlingly clear in our new power to bomb it all away in a nuclear fire storm (an accomplishment of male lack of conversion left to its solitary self!).

For the first time it will be men and women *together* who will have to save this also temporary, lovely earth of ours. And just in the nick of time! A sexual-spiritual mode of being in the world will save it because we will insist that earth's material beauty and goodness and our embodied selves are one. Together we will forbid anyone, any nation, any cartel, to blast away this earth, this part of ourselves—that Dante called this small round floor—that makes us passionate (feeling and suffering) and compassionate (suffering with one another and the earth). Holistic, sexual spirituality can end our deepest scandal: pretending we are separate as nations, races, or sexes and not one human race, one with the earth and with God.

Does this position rule out commitment? Not at all, because commitment itself must first be made to God and listening to God's voice through people, events, and things, and God's voice in who we are—the kind of gifts, limitations, strengths, and weaknesses that keep us in process of becoming. So I'm not recommending temporariness as opposed to commitment, but, instead, commitment as listening and following where God's Spirit leads us each day. That kind of commitment puts order into our lives and our loves, because neither sexuality nor spirituality can take over the personality. They remain, as they must, only dimensions, *functions*, expressions of who we are becoming. But always person is primary to any of those functions, for "person" is not confined by any function. Rather, we use them all, listening for the cues for the next scene, the next move to follow the Spirit.

That kind of commitment to listening to God's call compels us to *live in the present*, an important requirement for prayer and for peaceful, contemplative living as well. For accepting and fully living in the present delivers us, too, from the need to feel we must do everything, possess everything, compete with everyone. That commitment rests us in God for the few days and nights we spend in this world preparing for our transition into yet more intimacy with Him.

8

The Fifty-ninth Day

It seems that the water lily has amazing reproductive powers. One water lily is said to double overnight. A farmer setting out water lilies on his lake asked a friend if he could solve a riddle about the lilies. "You see," he said, "if they keep doubling every day and I want to fill my lake with these lilies within sixty days, when, my friend, will the lake be half full?"

His friend thought a long while, chewing on a straw, and then suddenly a grin broke through his thoughtful frown. "Why, of course, that's easy! The lake will be half full—it has to be—on the fifty-ninth day!"

The story of the water lily is full of meaning for all of us faced with the incredible challenges of these last decades of the twentieth century. Will the eighties and nineties—this unbelievable transition time for the race—quietly double and redouble the gifts, values, and contributions of woman so that woman and her healing partner, man, free at last, can glimpse the first red rays of humanity's new dawn: the fifty-ninth day?

The twenty-first century will see great emotional and moral change experiences as men and women learn to share in all the aspects of life. They will experience in themselves the dying and rising involved in God's call to reassess their social-sexual roles. If each Christian shares somewhat in Christ's crucifixion sometime in life, then this painful challenge to reevaluate their roles is a compliment God bestows on men, for one, in our time. Could God be asking men to design with Him the "new man" for the twenty-first century, one never seen before? God must feel men are equal to it. The invitation has been extended.

If men will go through these changes (having their consciousness raised), and learn to discover their own gifts—not "male" gifts but their personal gifts—male liberation can be even more exciting than women's. No longer will the male have to be the norm for the whole human race, an incredible relief!

Imagine with what joy this newly enlightened, liberated male will witness the creative genius of women, freed to use their gifts fully in the arts, literature, and music, given equal opportunities in the new Eden. Woman, now man's equal in self-concept, education, and opportunity, will at last carry out her part of the human task.

Woman in the twenty-first century? She will be liberated by her own efforts and the help of others. But she herself may have to be one of the greatest liberators in the world's history. For she will have to prophesy, to tell the truth about what she sees going on in the world: that the emperor has no clothes. She will have to say what she honestly feels and knows to be true about war, poverty, sexual-spiritual relationships, children, and especially, her own gifts.

Rising from an inferior to an equal position, women will, of course, be bothered by the usual temptations of any group (coming out of Egypt!) to copy their one-time oppressors.

> When those who feel themselves oppressed by social patterns begin to resist, they frequently attempt merely to move from one end of the axis to the other. Those who are dominated wish for themselves to become dominant. It's important to recognize such a movement constitutes *only a rebellion*, not a revolution. It does not herald a new age. A significant future will not be born until the *orientation of the axis itself has been shifted*. [emphasis added]
> —Beatrice Bruteau

What women want for the world is real revolution in its best sense of "new things." To prophesy and tell the truth in love will call for women serious and disciplined about training both intellect and imagination. Women cannot be content merely with wild charges against men, assumptions, and lack of evidence. They will be serious scholars, professionals, evokers of gifts—including their own as sexual-spiritual lovers.

Beatrice Bruteau calls this coming age in which communion
qualities will be practiced by all, "neofeminism," a consciousness concrete, integral, and unitive. Its goal will be to
nurture the uniqueness of all persons—their likenesses and
differences. Yet she says women in this neofeminist time will
not reject the agency qualities once attributed only to males:
clear reasoning, organization, and intellectual pursuits.

For a time it may be necessary to question some so-called
typical masculine values, especially those that thus far have produced war and poverty, demeaned the human person, and
wiped out human freedom. Formerly only those masculine vir-
tues such as loyalty to the male group, organizational power,
domination of other groups, ethical decisions divorced from
emotion, and, of course, the worship of power, received honor
in society. Those characteristics produced the nuclear bomb
and Hiroshima. If unchecked by female (and male!) prophecy
and conversion, the call to honesty, they will produce World
War III.

Feminist consciousness will look at these masculine contributions, evaluate them, consult with males about them, and
choose carefully the valuable from them. It will submit them to
the newly trained female mind and heart and produce a *human*
consciousness for a new world. As long ago as 1952, Eleanor
Roosevelt cited the need:

> I believe we will have better government when men and
> women discuss public issues together and make their
> decisions on the basis of their differing areas of concern for
> the welfare of their families and their world—*too often the*
> *great decisions are originated and given form in bodies*
> *made up wholly of men, or so completely dominated by*
> *them that whatever of special value women have to offer is*
> *shunted aside without expression.*

Human consciousness includes both male and female values. It works for unity and will discard forever the separation of
God and nature, body and spirit, male and female. We will do
that especially through synthesis, seeing each individual as a

uniquely precious set of gifts from God, a set of God's expectations for a holistic world.

Each of us is a vital unit in this plan for a future world, each of us as a separate chord in God's libretto. That attitude will imply a respect for studying the designer's score. Each of us needs, then, to be read, understood, cherished, and integrated into the total symphony that calls for their particular song.

We'll effectively challenge the double standard, that dual sex ethic, and declare it both dishonest and morally wrong, an injustice to both male and female ideals of honest loving. We will call sexism what it is: immoral.

As friends of Jesus we are not necessarily equal in talent, but we are all equal before God: whole persons with our own gifts. Especially the gift that we *are*. Human consciousness will work for acceptance of this precious gift of "presence" from one another as fellow humans. That attitude will refuse to categorize people as non-Christian, nonmale, nonwhite, nonfree. As God's ideas, people will be respected for their humanity, not as male or female, not because of sexual orientation, for these categories will end. In fact, such classifications will no longer apply! They may well become just as archaic as nationality in a world finally one united planet of people helping one another to be fed, housed, educated, and healed.

One of the spiritual obstacles to this vision we've seen above: that theology of arrogance produced by male pride that relegated women to an inferior category and did not see sex and spirit as equal dimensions of healthy human activity.

We need also to remove some psychological obstacles, such as the irrational fear of the gay-lesbian orientation. Understanding the psychological process that produces *homophobia* is important, for this disease is close cousin to the wild panic that produced the Nazi Holocaust against European Jews. Its roots lie in that same dragon we've seen so often in these pages, the fear of difference! That fear is as culturally conditioned as the theology that tries to respond to it. Human behavior different from the "normal" inspires notice, then resentment and fear. Especially fear of the challenge to one's own behavior, ideas, and practices.

But even more dangerous is the child of this irrational fear
and panic, intolerance. We can't permit this different behavior
because it challenges our self-image, our moral stance, our religious beliefs perhaps. So, we strike back. The infamous Nazi
Night of the Broken Glass was just such a pogrom, an explosion
of fear, panic, and blind intolerance against the Jewish scapegoat
who dared to be different (some Germans believed) from them.
Now the panic explodes over race; again, over sex; again, over
sexual lifestyle; again, over religious difference!

We may want to relegate this sort of thing to Nazism or the
Ku Klux Klan, but so strong is that intolerance called homophobia that through the years right here in what is now the
United States, gays and lesbians have been executed for their
sexual orientation. In 1776, the death penalty awaited any
convicted homosexual; the last execution for such was in Philadelphia in 1780.

The statutes of Massachusetts, significantly, condemned
homosexuals by invoking the Christian Scripture, especially
Leviticus 18:22, 20:13 and Romans 1:26-27. Some exegetes
today feel that these passages don't necessarily contain a con-
demnation of gay-lesbian behavior in a loving, caring relationship, but are culturally conditioned pieces of advice.

This irrational fear of homosexuality is part fear of the body
itself and its sexual powers. How can we condemn homosexuality until we understand more about sexuality? I recommend
an international, interdisciplinary, inter-religious study of all
the dimensions of sexuality as an integral part of our humanity.
At least the results of such a study might give us somewhat
adequate data to undergird our views of what constitutes *normal*
human sexual behavior. It might even affect some theological
approaches to what constitutes *moral* sexual behavior.

If each human person is friend of God and of other human
persons, we'll repudiate the present economic system that uses
and exploits one group of people, the poor, for the profit of
another. That social structure of haves and have-nots must
change so that the new human consciousness will pervade
society.

As this new consciousness grows, some prophets, truth-tellers, will point out that boundary lines between countries, lines on maps, are not carved in cement. These lines are a lie, even a heresy. What will an idea like nationality mean in the face of loving human consciousness? Challenged to look deeper at the real humans who make up countries, we'll see only fellow lovers, for we are one people on one endangered planet, who must cling together and work to supply our mutual needs of food, clothing, shelter, and education.

Edmund J. Egan gives the name heterosexual consciousness to the model he'd like to see us use to help solve our moral crisis, especially the dual sex ethic and the split between will and emotion. However, I still prefer the term *human* consciousness as more inclusive, especially because of our gay and lesbian sisters and brothers who might feel excluded.

Regardless of the term used, Egan has some questions that will have to be answered if we want to develop that new consciousness:

- Can consumer capitalism survive the end of specialized aggressive conduct among men?
- Can consumer capitalism survive the end of compulsive buying and hoarding patterns among women?
- Will the new respectability of gentleness among men make it easy to raise armies?
- As vision and feeling cease to be termed issues of mere sentiment . . . will we continue to tolerate the crippling effects of ugliness in our cities, our art, our entertainment, our lives?
- As regards sexuality itself, may not the termination of the oldest master-slave relationship give rise to possible friendship between men and women, and consequently, a new community among us all?

Conversion for the twenty-first century is a radical call to radical love that will cut to the bone. That new life—the putting on of the attitudes and values of Jesus—can lead to this human consciousness to which conversion calls us. We can translate that goal into reality as we go through the various conversions we still need en route! This consciousness based on the most radical of all loves, that found most clearly in Jesus' attitudes in the gospel, can implement his values. Those values stand as the epitome of what it means to be human.

That human consciousness, of course, is still a sight unseen. No generation of people within our history has yet experienced this male-female accepting, unprejudiced consciousness. Men and women have never at any time in history related to one another as intellectual, moral, biological, and spiritual equals—until these faint beginnings in our time. Herein lies the difficulty—and worth—of the work ahead of us. The actual words of a woman realizing the difficulty of that task for her are poignant:

> Being female and feminine has meant to me a lot of things. And they've had lots of positive and negative aspects to them.
>
> I remember when my brother got a car. I complained bitterly and my parents pointed out that Jim paid for the car with his own money. I, equally reasonably, pointed out that he earned the money by work that was not open to me as a female.
>
> Being feminine means *waiting*—waiting for the phone to ring, for a date, for babies to arrive, in carpool lines, in doctors' offices, for life to happen! When you wait, you don't have to stick your neck out, run risks, and risk rejection, but you are also not in charge of your own destiny.
>
> Being feminine means being *protected*. I was handed over—literally—into the protective custody of one man to another, my father to my husband. I was 37 years old before I slept alone in a house—and loved the solitude. Being protected financially and physically has disadvantages. You don't have to worry. But you also have to accept being treated as a child—as someone not capable of taking care of herself.

Being feminine means being *functionalized*. I have been date, wife, mother, cook, cleaning lady, chauffeur, etc. But rarely have I felt valued just because I'm myself. Playing a role is easy. You never have to worry about what you're going to do, but you also never discover who you are.

Being feminine means being a *manipulator*. I can't even remember when I learned to manipulate, but I know I unconsciously do it. Manipulating does get results and you don't have to risk frontal assault—but it requires an enormous amount of energy and it *is* degrading.

Being feminine means being *invisible* and often inaudible as well. It means being ignored in male conversation or sitting silently in the back of the classroom. Again nothing is risked but nothing is gained.

Finally, being feminine means being *trivialized*—being "just a housewife," "just like a woman." My alltime favorite and often repeated insult is: "Do you work or are you just a housewife?" I remember the head of the theology department at Gannon College saying they needed more men in the graduate program because women weren't interested in real theology—only in "fluff"—and then when I asked to write my thesis on theology of the Nazi holocaust, was told that it wasn't an appropriate subject for a woman (so I became devious and did it anyway). If you are trivial you don't have to take yourself seriously—but no one else will either.

I realize as I write this that it sounds very negative and, in fact, my basic orientation is not negative. I like being female and there are many things about being feminine that I enjoy. But perhaps the negative must be exorcized before the positive can be accentuated again.

—P. Randolph

This kind of awareness and realization is not the exclusive experience of women on the road to human consciousness. Men are making giant steps in awareness of the damage done to

their own self-concepts and of the pressures society exerts on
them to be masculine, if not macho. Great news for everyone.
Because we will never achieve human consciousness without
men and women working as friends in the effort toward our
mutual liberation.

Both women and men will have to be warriors of human
consciousness and mighty prayer warriors, listening to their
hearts and God's. Saying no to war, world hunger, national
greed, oppression, prisons, slums, juvenile halls, child prostitution. These are the real enemies—not some so-called "foreign"
nation.

A healed sexual self-image will help us see one another as
partners fighting this primary battle, attacking these universal
enemies, breaking down ancient barriers, and using our money, time, and energy in a battle worthy of our humanity.

The maimed male self-image will at last escape from the pain
of playing soldier century after century when women had no
power to say him nay. All war must end, the great battle standards
packed away. The real warfare must begin: We must fight to save
our environment, our children, our humanity, our planet.

In the drama ahead we'll find the road to free responsible
choice through, and not in spite of, accepting our sexuality as
good gift. The approach of the New Testament—"In Christ
there is neither male nor female" (Galatians 3:28)—calls us
beyond sex distinctions to a holistic spirituality that both
embraces and transcends our sexuality. To fulfill and develop
this spirituality as a mature relationship with God, neighbor,
and self, we ask how can we develop such a unique, personal
spirituality, so different from society's expectations. We can do
it. Working with God and others, we can experience the broad
sensuous sweep of our sexuality, its power, its beauty, its challenge to live as responsible lovers.

Each of us, a precious individual personality, fashions a
sexual spirituality that mirrors the unity of this immersion in
life and its joyous acceptance, balanced always by our deepening love life in prayer.

Yet male/female sexuality remains an area of ambiguity. We

know so little about woman as fully human. So we have so
many unfounded assumptions to discard about her. We see
woman's body in all the media as the perennial sex object. Yet
we also see sexuality used to express profound love and friendship. How shall we, how can we, break through those ancient
barriers? How will we speak across the dreadful years?

To express our heart's meaning and our love, we need to see
each other afresh, through new lenses. Without male-female
communication sending and receiving meaning, it will be hard
to develop such a sexual spirituality. Yet our mutual liberation
hangs on that attempt to communicate. In study, discussion,
loving, sharing—and also in the deepest form of communication, prayer for and with one another—women and men can let
the Spirit teach us our truest identity: *that we are beloved.* We
invite God to knock down the walls, melt the ancient stereotypes, and gift us with those new glasses.

That challenge to communicate is for both sexes the Spirit's
call to conversion. New glasses can be painful as well. Our own
faces will be clearer in the glass as we acquire this God's-eye
view of one another. We'll learn so much and discard so much.
One woman tells how much she learned about her own sexual
relations with her husband, how much they both suffered from
false expectations and foolish ideas. It took twenty-seven years
of marriage, study, prayer, and therapy; but they worked it
through, and they are now freed, happy people.

Women and men are now engaged in the task of discarding
role stereotypes about each other. Anatomy will not be destiny;
a female body does not necessarily imply wifehood or moth-
erhood; nor need every male be husband or father. When we
accept one another as equally human, unlimited possibilities
and their social implications stretch before us.

Now engaged in the greatest social and theological revolution in history, we're trying to change not merely a government,
but the very fundamental attitudes of the human race. Woman,
the Sleeping Beauty, will awaken to power; how will she wield
it? As women follow God's call to radical love, using power well
is part of that call. We can discover that God's call does not

presuppose "success," but a transformed humanity.

We humans sometimes think we are here on earth for the work, when all the time the work is here for us. God provides it as the means of our growing in understanding, compassion, and radical love. We work seriously and well, but with light hearts, our eyes on the deeper process of becoming lovers.

Together women and men will take responsibility for that most real of human tasks, learning how to become lovers. We don't know yet what that will look like because women and men have never before been equal partners in the project. But God knows and is waiting on tiptoe for that beautiful sight of her sons and daughters coming into their own.

That new humanity will *look* different, too, because, for the first time, woman is becoming free to share her vision of what a transformed world should look like. First, because through biological research she now exercises control over human reproduction, with consequent responsibility for valid choices in that regard. Secondly, because she how has some small access to real decision making. Eventually, coproductive and coresponsible with man, she will have to codecide for the human race.

Women and men help fulfill this responsibility if they accept the task of developing the radical love that can carry them through any task, political, social, or personal. Responding to that challenge, no longer crippled by inferiority and its false images of self and God, the human race can use our full potential, walking at last on *two* sound legs.

A call to radical love, to accept others in their radical act of being themselves, implies the freedom to answer. So sexual spirituality looks to Jesus as the model of a free humanity. Once freed by his values, we can answer, can move to complete God's plan for free beings. No longer need the male alone provide all the knowledge, power, and gifts for the world. Woman, no longer surrogate human, no longer servant but friend, can then cocreate the world with man to the Designer's fairly obvious specifications.

An idea like sexual spirituality may have seemed an incredible assumption to some readers, but breaking through society's expectations in this area will be rewarding if we involve our total person in our love life, even to making love with God. All lovemaking will be better once we discard those false sexual fables, guilt trips, and immature notions about God. We can change, others can change, and so can the world.

Women and men together will see that, after all, spirit has always had a lot to do with sex, and vice versa. Finally, sexual spirituality can help carry us glowing with love into the heart of God. It empowers us to say to human, and God Lover, "I love you as I am; human, needy, dependent—and with my body, my myself, I thee worship."

> And so it came to pass that some of these created ones were
> chosen—
> Were given extra love for others from God's love.
> Were given lightness of feet and the rhythm of the trees,
> the wind, the deer in the forests and the flowers on their
> stems
> were given a caring for music to comfort the weeping,
> to dance by, and to clap their hands
> were given words and lights and understanding to speak
> for God and of God, to find their way and help others,
> and to lead and to follow.

> And some of these were women,
> not by mistake, but by design,
> not to be second-rate, but to be best, too—
> not because men need women, but because God needs
> women.
>
> —F. Fairhill

And some of them are men!—who together with their new-found friend, woman, will fulfill the words of Isaiah:

> They that wait upon the Lord shall renew their strength;
> They shall mount up with wings as eagles;
> They shall run and not be weary;
> They shall walk and not grow faint.
>
> —Isaiah 40:31

Resources and References

Aquinas, Thomas, St., *Scriptum Super Sententiis*, III, Dist. 27, Q. 2, a. 1.

————— , *Summa Theologiae*, II-II, Q. 23, a. 1.

Augustine of Hippo, St., *The Confessions*, John K. Ryan, trans., Garden City, N.Y., Doubleday Image, 1960.

Bachofen, J. J., *Myth, Religion and Mother Right*, Princeton, N.J., Princeton University Press, 1967.

Bakan, David, *And They Took Themselves Wives*, New York/San Francisco, Harper & Row, 1979.

Bell, Alan P. and Martin S. Weinberg, *Homosexualities*, New York, Simon and Schuster, 1978.

Berger, Peter, *The Social Reality of Religion*, London, Faber & Faber, 1969.

Berry, Thomas, "Classical Western Spirituality and the American Experience," *Cross Currents*, Winter 1981-82.

Block, Jeanne, "Conceptions of Sex Role: . . .," *American Psychologist*, vol. 28 (1973).

Boyd, Malcomb, *Take Off the Masks*, Philadelphia, New Society Publishers, 1984.

Branden, Nathaniel, *The Disowned Self*, New York, Bantam, 1973.

Bruteau, Beatrice, "Feminine and Masculine Consciousness," *Cross Currents*, Summer 1977.

Buber, Martin, *I and Thou*, Walter Kaufman, trans., New York, Scribner, 1970.

Bullough, Vern and Bonnie, *The Subordinate Sex*, New York, Penguin, 1974.

Callwood, June, *Love, Hate, Fear, Anger, and the Other Lively Emotions*, San Bernardino, Calif., Borgo Press, 1980.

Clark, Elizabeth and Herbert Richardson, *Women and Religion*, New York, Harper & Row, 1976.

Daly, Mary, *Beyond God the Father*, Boston, Beacon Press, 1973.

David, Elizabeth Gould, *The First Sex*, New York, Putnam, 1971.

Davis, Charles, *Body as Spirit*, New York, Seabury, 1976.

De Beauvoir, Simone, *The Second Sex*, New York, Random House, 1974.

DeRougement, Denis, *Love in the Western World*, Princeton, N.J., Princeton University Press, 1983.

Deschene, James, "Sexuality: Festival of the Spirit," *Studies in Formative Spirituality*, vol. II, no. 1, February 1981.

Doherty, Sr. Austin, "Is There a Psychology of Women?" Grailville Women's Seminar.

Donnelly, Dody H., *Team*, New York, Paulist Press, 1977.

——————, "The Sexual Mystic," *The Feminist Mystic*, Crossroad, New York, 1982.

Egan, Edmund, "The Transformation of Ethics and Heterosexual Consciousness," *Cross Currents*, Summer 1973.

Everson, William, *River-root/A Syzygy*, Oyez Press, 1976.

Feldman, Alan, *The Happy Genius*, New York, Sun Press, 1978.

Ferguson, Charles, *The Male Attitude*, Boston, Little Brown, 1966.

Fontinell, Eugene, "Immortality: Hope or Hindrance?" *Cross Currents*, Summer 1981.

Fox, Douglas, "The Alien Generation," *Spiritual Life Magazine*, Spring 1966.

Gelpi, Donald, *Charism and Sacrament*, New York, Paulist, 1977.

Gilligan, Carol, *In a Different Voice*, Cambridge, Mass., Harvard University Press, 1983.

Goergen, Donald, *Sexual Celibate*, New York, Seabury, 1975.

Gollwitzer, Helmut, Keith Krim, trans., *Song of Love*, New York, Fortress, 1979.

Hadewijch: The Complete Works, Mother Columba Hart, trans., New York, Paulist, 1981.

Haughton, Rosemary, *Love*, Baltimore, Penguin, 1971.

Hays, H. R., *The Dangerous Sex*, New York, Putnam, 1964.

"Homosexuality and Social Justice," Report of the Task Force on Gay/Lesbian Issues, Commission on Social Justice, Archdiocese of San Francisco, 1982.

Human Sexuality: A Roman Catholic Study, New York, Paulist, 1977.

Human Sexuality: A United Church of Christ Study, New York, United Church Press, 1977.

Human Sexuality: Contemporary Perspectives, Eleanor Morrison and V. Borosage, eds., 2nd ed., Palo Alto, Calif., 1977.

James, William, *Varieties of Religious Experience*, New York, New American Library, 1958.

Kazantzakis, Nikos, Kimor Friar, trans., *Saviors of God*, New York, Simon & Schuster Touchstone Books, 1959.

Knitter, Paul, "Merton's Eastern Remedy for Christianity's Anonymous Dualism," *Cross Currents*, Fall 1981.

Laeuchli, Samuel, *Power and Sexuality: The Emergence of Canon Law at the Synod of Elvira*, Philadelphia, Temple University Press, 1972.

Lebel, Robert, "Sex-Differentiation . . .," unpublished manuscript, Madison, Wisc., 1980.

Lowen, Alexander, *The Betrayal of the Body*, New York, Collier-Macmillan, 1969.

Maccoby, Eleanor, "What We Know and Don't Know About Sex-Difference," *Psychology Today*, Dec. 1974.

Maguire, Daniel, "Human Sexuality . . .," *Proceedings of the Catholic Theological Society of America*, vol. 33, 1978.

May, Rollo, *Love and Will*, New York, Dell, 1973.

McGrath, Sr. A. Magnus, O.P., *Woman and the Church*, New York, Image Books, 1976.

Merton, Thomas, *Contemplative Prayer*, New York, Doubleday, 1971.

Milhaven, John G., "Sex and Love and Marriage . . .," *National Catholic Reporter*, 13 January 1978, p. 7.

Moore, Sebastian, unpublished study, Milwaukee, Marquette University, 1979.

Morris, Joan, *The Lady Was a Bishop*, New York, Macmillan, 1973.

Nelson, James B., *Embodiment*, Minneapolis, Augsburg, 1979.

O'Neill, John, *The Church and the Homosexual*, New York, Sheed, Andrews, 1978.

Padavano, Anthony, "Religious Experience," *Diaspora*, Jan. 1980.

Pittenger, Norman, *Making Sexuality Human*, New York, Pilgrim Press, 1979.

Raming, Ida, *The Exclusion of Women from the Priesthood: Divine Law or Sex Discrimination?*, Metuchen, N.J., Scarecrow Press, 1976.

Rausch, Jerome, *Agape and Amicitia*, Rome, Catholic Book Agency, 1958.

Ricoeur, Paul, "Sexuality and the Modern Word," *Cross Currents*, Winter 1975.

Roszak, Betty and Theodore, *Masculine-Feminine*, New York, Harper & Row, 1970.

Ruether, Rosemary, *New Woman-New Earth*, New York, Seabury, 1978.

Stone, Merlin, *When God Was a Woman*, New York, Harcourt Brace Jovanovich, 1978.

Teresa of Avila: The Interior Castle, Kieran Kavanaugh and Otilio Rodrigues, trans., New York, Paulist, 1979.

Toner, Jules, *What Is Love?*, Washington, D.C., Corpus, 1968.

Tripp, C. A., *Homosexual Matrix*, New York, New American Library, 1976.

Watts, Alan W., *Nature, Man and Woman*, New York, Random House, 1970.

Williams, Daniel D., *The Spirit and the Forms of Love*, Lanham, Md., University Press of America, 1981.

Woods, Richard, *Another Kind of Love: Homosexuality and Spirituality*, New York, Doubleday, 1978.

Zilbergeld, Bernie, *Male Sexuality*, New York, Bantam, 1978.

Index